AF531368

ANXIETY BEHAVIOUR IN CHILDREN

ANXIETY BEHAVIOUR IN CHILDREN

By

V.V BHARATHI

DISCOVERY PUBLISHING HOUSE PVT. LTD.
NEW DELHI-110 002

Edition – 2017

ISBN: 978-81-7141-181-8

Anxiety Behaviour in Children

Published by:

DISCOVERY PUBLISHING HOUSE PVT. LTD.
4383/4B, Ansari Road Darya Ganj
New Delhi - 110 002 (India)
Phone: +91-11-23279245, 43596064-65
Fax: +91-11-23253475
E-mail: discoverypublishinghouse@gmail.com
sales@discoverypublishinggroup.com
web: www.discoverypublishinggroup.com

Printed at:
Infinity Imaging Systems
Delhi

Foreword

I am extremely pleased to see the research work of Dr. (Mrs.) V.V. Bharathi, being published in the form of a book for a wider readership.

The book presents the research work on anxiety in elementary school children and comprises of a well designed study of select antecedent and consequent variables. The causes, manifestation and handling of anxiety behaviour in children, are not completely understood and skillfully managed by the concerned. Dr. (Mrs.) Bharathi has accomplished through her research probe new information about the operation and antecedents of anxiety behaviour of young children. The crucial role of family structure and tension balance between parents, parental attitudes and speech and language functions have been clearly established. While studies on anxiety behaviour of young children are negligibly few, Dr. Bharathi's findings reported in this book will surely evoke keen interest among the research scholars in the field, for further research. It also emerges from the study, the need for parent education programme in our country and refinement of the techniques of handling anxiety behaviour by recognising the relevant antecedent and consequent variables throughly discussed in this book. On the whole, this is a comprehensive source of information on anxiety and a critical review of literature on anxiety research. I am sure all those interested in this field of research, as well as the students of

Human Development and Family Studies, Psychology, and social work, teachers and research scholars will find this book a valuable source material for consultation.

I wish the author, all the best and look forward to see her publishing many more works of this type.

Prof. S.R. Venkatramaiah
M.A., Ph.D., D.M.P., F.I. A.C.P.
Professor of Clinical Psychology,
Department of Home Science

Preface

This book is based on my Doctoral Thesis on anxiety in school children—A study of certain antecedent and consequent behavioural correlates. This is an extremely important problem. The importance of anxiety as a powerful influence in the present day civilization is acknowledged by all. It has become an essential part of modern civilization and premeate all spheres of life. Yet anxiety is a highly unpleasant state of tension which the in dividual wants to get rid off.

Research on anxiety has been scant in India. Cultural setting being an important factor in anxiety, it is of highest importance that anxiety to be studied in different cultural settings and the resultant behaviour of children. Since the present research has given equal importance to both antecedent and consequent behaviour, it proves relevant information to parents, teachers, social workers and other experts who work with young children.

I am greatly indebted to Prof. S.R. Venkatramaiah for having given me the necessary inspiration and advise besides guiding the thesis. My heartfelt thanks are to my family members without whose cooperation I would not have been able to complete this project. My special thanks are due to all children and their parents and the heads of various schools without whose cooperation this study would have been impossible.

Author

Acknowledgements

It is great pleasure to acknowledge the kind help and suggestions given by the persons mentioned below in preparing the thesis.

Dr. S.R. Venkatramaiah, Reader in Clinical Psychology, Department of Home Science, S.V.U. College was my thesis supervisor. To him I remain grateful and indebted, for, he gave me an opportunity to work on the topic of my thesis and further enthused me to develop critical thinking in that area of research. I have tried to imbibe from him the value of precision, skill and measured expression which he always insisted upon and regarded as very important in scientific reporting. It is his suggestion, criticism and advice that improved immeasurably the research reported in all its aspects.

My sincere thanks and appreciation are due to Professor (Miss) P.R. Reddy, Professor and Head of the Department of Home Science, S.V.U. College, for having encouraged me to join as a part time research scholar in the department and for helping me by giving practical suggestions.

I must remember and thank Dr. (Mrs.) K. Rajeswari Murthy (Presently at Amsterdam, New York) the then Principal, S.P.W. College who encouraged me to do research in the University as a part time research scholar. It is my good fortune that all the subsequent principals continued to provide encouragement and facilities throughout my research tenure. Particularly I should mention Miss K.P. Kamala Menon, who is the Principal of S.P.W. College for providing necessary administrative support and personal encouragement for completing the research programme. Mrs. Maria Teresita, Head of the Department of Home Science, S.P.W. College deserves my thanks for helping me to complete the research work.

I offer my grateful thanks to Mrs. V. Vijayalakshmi, the Statistician, Department of Home Science, S.V.U. College for advising me in the statistical analysis of the data. But for her support it would not have been possible for me to understand and complete the analysis.

The factor analysis of the subscales on PARI was made easy, by Sri P. Subba Reddy, Research Scholar, Department of Computer Science, Indian Institute of Technology, Guindy, Madras. The entire data was processed on the IBM System 370 computer with the help of Sri P. Subba Reddy. I specially thank him for his services.

In successfully completing my research, I needed information and permission for visiting various elementary schools in Tirupati (both municipal schools and privately managed schools). I must thank the Commissioner, Tirupati Municipality and the Correspondents of private management schools for providing all the facilities I required.

I appreciate and offer my thanks to all the small children, whom I approached for collection of data. They responded favourably to my demands and put up with long sessions I had with them. They deserve my heart felt thanks. It is needless for me to say how important that cooperation from the teachers of the respective schools I visited, was in successfully completing the task of data collection. They not only helped me during my work with children but also in locating the houses of children in my sample. To all of them, I owe my sincere thanks.

In the preparation of the thesis the specifications and recommendations of the style format in the thesis composition made by American Psychological Association Publication Manual (1976) were incorporated.

V.V. BHARATHI

Contents

List of Abbreviations

ANOVA	: Analysis of Variance
CMAS	: Children's Manifest Anxiety Scale
cf	: Cumulative Frequency
DCL	: Dream Check List
f	: Frequency
FS & TBQ	: Family Structure and Tension Balance Questionnaire
HA	: High Anxiety
LA	: Low Anxiety
NS	: Not Significant
NW	: Number of Words
SEC	: Socio-economic Status
SCL	: Social Class Levels
SQ	: Syntax Quotient
TC	: Total Correct
TE	: Total Errors
TO	; Total Omissions
TS	: Total Sentences
TU	: Total Unit
TW	: Total Words
WPS	: Words Per Sentence
PARI	: Parental Attitude Research Instrument

List of Figures

List of Tables

1

Introduction

Perhaps no other concept is so thoroughly discussed and extensively studied by behavioural scientists as is ***anxiety***. No one can dispute the fact that it is the central explanatory concept in almost all contemporary theories of personality. However, attempts to incorporate explanations within a single psychological framework have not been entirely successful, because of diverse conditions which act as antecedent variables leading to a wide variety of manifestation.

Anxiety is ***protean*** in its nature. Speilberger (1966) quotes the following passage from *Time* (March 31, 1961 p. 44) which well supports the universality of the appearance of anxiety and its powerful influence in contemporary life;

> "Anxiety seems to be the dominant fact—and is threatening to become the dominant *cliche*—of modern life. It shouts from head lines, laughs nervously from cocktail parties, nags from advertisement, speaks suavely in the board room, whines from the stage, clatters from the Wall Street ticker jokes with fake youthfulness in the golf course and whispers in privacy everyday before the shaving mirror and the dressing table. Not merely the

black statistics of murder, suicide, alcoholism and divorce betray anxiety (or the special form of anxiety, which is guilt), but almost innocent any everyday act; the limp or overhearty handshake, the second pack of cigarettes or third martini, the forgotten appointment, the stammer in the mid-sentence, the wasted hour before the T. V. Set, the spanked child, the new car unpaid for".

The wholesale attack on the concept of anxiety in the past, seems to have been principally to assess, a broad spectrum of behavioural correlates *and or* to test specific predictions from a general theoretical framework. For example, the work of Spence and Taylor, (1953); and Malmo (1957) illustrates the point. In this process, a good majority of the work was on adult human subjects. This leaves certain important issues and questions unattacked. To cite a few; how does anxiety typically express itself in the behaviour of children? Is there a difference either qualitative or quantitative in the pattern of anxiety behaviour between adults and children? To what extent the anxiety behaviour is influenced by the socio-cultural factors? What specific areas of behaviour are invariably affected in children? Little is known about the intrafamilial variables such as parental attitudes, family structure etc., which possibly get causatively involved in the development and manifestations of anxiety in early childhood. These are some of the questions and issues which arise in an enquiry into the antecedent and consequent behavioural correlates of anxiety in young children. The problem and the scope of the present thesis is largely confined to some of the questions and issues referred to above.

Some Issues in the Meaning and Definition of Anxiety

A brief treatment of the concept of anxiety is necessary at the outset. Almost every one agrees that anxiety is an 'unpleasant feeling state' clearly distinguishable from other emotional states and is having psychological concomitants.

Although interest in anxiety phenomena has historical background in the Philosophical and Theological views of some European Philosophers and theologians it was Freud (1933) who seriously attempted to explain the meaning of anxiety. Anxiety to mind is as pain is to body. '*Angst*' is the term used by Freud in the context of psychic pain. According to him it is something felt, an unpleasant affective state or condition. A critical analysis of the literature, reveals what may be called three distinct approaches to the problem of anxiety viz., *psychoanalytical, behavioural* and *psychometric*. A brief account of these approaches is presented in the following pages.

Psychoanalytical Approaches

Freud describes a developmental point of view of anxiety by inquiring into the nature of early life experiences which could be called 'prototypical experiences' of anxiety in later years. According to his speculation, certain early universal experiences beginning at birth itself emerge leading to a state of *anxiety-preparedness*. We notice in these speculations an indication of biological roots of anxiety which is nothing, but a condition of increased sensory and motor attention. Though highly involved, this view point has been very seriously considered by later psychoanalytical investigators. Freud, subsequently mentions *three* types of anxiety or 'psychic pain':

(a) *reality anxiety*, arising when the individual is confronted by dangers or threats in the external world;

(b) *neurotic* anxiety, arising when the individuals Id impulses threaten to break through the ego controls and results in behaviour that will lead to his punishment; and

(c) *moral anxiety*, arising when the individual does something or even contemplates doing something in conflict with his super ego or moral values and arouses feelings of guilt.

Alfred Adler (1952), one of the Trinities of classical psychoanalysis, expalined anxiety in terms of arousal of inferiority feelings. Such feelings of inferiority are universal and are always compensated by constant strivings on the part of the individual. When compensations are partial or unsuccessful, anxiety manifests in the form of specific behavioural styles.

Among the neo-psychoanalytical approaches, the contributions of O. Rank (1952) and H. S. Sullivan (1940) perhaps are relevant to our main focus of interest. In their theoretical analysis there is greater recognition of the social and cultural determinants, and are concerned with the interpersonal relations among people in the immediate family environment.

The central idea in Rank's theory is the concept of birth-truma. Trumatic events of birth and separation from the mother. What becomes important therefore, is the feelings of security and any threat to such feelings of security will arouse anxiety. It may be seen that the threats to security of a person may arise from life experiences in the immediate family environment particularly so in the case of a child.

Sullivan (1940) emphasizes interaction between personality development and culture. The central concept in this theory is interpersonal relationships. He argues that an individual is to be understood only within the context of his family, friendships and social groups. According to him, the child in the process of acculturation experiences frequent conflicts between need satisfaction and security. As parents use prohibitions and disapproval in the acculturation process, anxiety manifests itself primarily due to the child's anticipated inability to fulfil these expectations.

Behavioural Approach

The behavioural approach is deeply base on the need to study behaviour objectively by examining the nature of the stimuli acting on the organism and the nature of its responses. In this approach the mediating processes do not receive much attention. The basic concepts and their derivative principles have emerged from the fundamental works of Pavlov, Watson, Skinner, Mowrer, Hull, Spence and Taylor and Niller and Dollard, who have established themselves as behavioural scientists. Disregarding certain minor variations, the behavioural approach as a whole emphasizes that anxiety behaviour is learned, within the general frame of the principles of learning processes. By and large anxiety has come to be viewed by this group of psychologists as *conditioned emotional response*.

Psychometric (Factor analytical) Approach

Factor analytical approach may be otherwise called psychometric approach and is a contrast to other approaches discussed above in terms of inclusiveness and systematic theory building. But they have the marked advantage of a precise formulation based on empirical measurements. Anxiety as an aspect of personality is viewed as a system of interdependent traits or factors. Making use of the factor analytical methods attempts are made to build a model of the structure of anxiety in terms of test scores, traits, dimensions, first and second order factors. Attractive as it is, this psychometric approach has become a major tenet in psychological analysis of basic concepts. Using a factor analytical approach applied to data from questionnaires, life history reports, and laboratory investigations, Cattell finds (1966) a relatively broad, second order factors which he identifies as anxiety. This factor correlates with psychiatric ratings of anxiety. differentiates neurotics, but not psychotics from normals, showing a reduction following therapy, rises in normals as they encounter threats and uncertainties, shows a U-shaped function from adolescence to old age, varies directly with economic insecurity and lack of cultural integrat on in cross cultural studies, and is associated with increase in general autonomic activity, such as high serum cholinesterase, high skin conductance, and increased heart rate.

Concepts which appear to be related to anxiety but factorially distinct are 'effort-stress', 'general excitement' or 'arousal', and 'fear', which is viewed as a 'motive state' or 'erg', associated with escape behaviour. General excitement is the broadest of the factors. Cattell offers two definitions of anxiety. The one which he believes is best supported by his data is, that, anxiety is a function of the magnitude of all unfulfilled needs (or ergs) and the degree of uncertainty that they will be fulfilled, or more simply stated anxiety corresponds to uncertainty of reward or total need fulfilment. The second definition about which he has some doubt is that anxiety is specific to the fear erg, and results from threat that occurs when there is anticipation of deprivation of any or all ergs.

It is noteworthy that Cattell distinguishes among fear as a motive state, general arousal or excitement, and anxiety which differs from the others, in that, it is associated with uncertainty and anticipation with regard to unfulfilled needs or values. It is of interest that Cattell further notes that anxiety is fostered by lack of integration, by an inability to focus upon external fears and by the existence of incompatible needs (Epstein, 1972).

Current Conceptualizations

From out of the large and massive data on anxiety accumulated over the past several decades, we begin to see attempts to develop neat conceptualization of the nature of anxiety and its measurement. We shall present a brief summary of some of the recent trends.

A Trait-State Conception of Anxiety

This has clarified certain ambiguities in the conceptual status of anxiety. Research findings have pointed out a necessity for the meaningful distinction between anxiety as a transitory 'state' and as a relatively stable personality 'trait'.

The next logical step is to differentiate between anxiety states, the stimulus conditions that evoke them and defenses that protect the individual. There is a general agreement that anxiety states are characterized by subjective, consciously perceived feelings of apprehension and tension accompanied by or associated with activation or arousal of autonomic nervous system. Anxiety as a *personality trait* is considered to imply a motive or acquired behavioural disposition that predisposes an individual to perceive a wide range of objectively non-dangerous events as threatening. In such circumstances the individual responds disproportionately to the magnitude of the objectively perceived danger. This conceptualization is not a theory of anxiety, but brings clarity to the measurement and description. In essence this distinction puts a widely differing research data into a framework. That is to say, the state concept requires a sequence of temporarily ordered events, in order to arouse anxiety. This process may be initiated by an external stimulus or an internal cue. If the stimulus situation is cognitively appraised as dangerous or threatening, then anxiety state reaction is produced. Further this reaction may initiate a behavioural sequence designed to avoid or deal directly with the dangerous situation. The trait concept on the other hand is assumed to reflect residues of past experience which determine individual differences in anxiety proneness. Such experiences which have most influence on the level of anxiety trait, is believed to date back to early childhood involving parent-child relationship particularly related to punishment situations.

From the stand point of this conceptualization at once it becomes important to clearly define the most important stimuli which are likely to produce different levels of anxiety states in individuals who differ in anxiety trait. This needs to be further explored.

Anxiety as a Drive

Based mostly on learning theory and its derivative models, the Drive theory proposes to fit in experimental data on the effects of anxiety on performance within the framework of Hullian postulates (1943). Briefly stated, the theory assumes that anxiety acts as a drive. There are important individual differences in the emotional responsiveness that contribute to the drive level (D). The total effective drive state results from the summation of all individual need states existent at a given time irrespective of the given source. The number and strength of specific habits is determined by subjects' previous experience. All habit tendencies evoke in the subject multiplied by the total effective drive then operating. This means higher the drive, greater the value of the response strength (Taylor and Spence, 1953).

Measurement of Anxiety—McReynold Scheme

It is now clear that anxiety is not merely a simple variable but rather represents several quite distinct dimensions. What is important is, to recognise fundamental modalities in the measurement techniques, so that the ambiguities are resolved. For example, we should construct tests for a specific meaningful measurement of anxiety rather than to determine what aspects of anxiety are measured by the tests already available. It appears there are a total of 88 formal anxiety measurement procedures pointing out to a less satisfactory status of anxiety assessment technology. McReynolds (1968) has conceptualized six dichotomous points of potential types of anxiety scores corresponding to the three dimensions of a cube. What is attempted here is to represent inter-relationships among different anxiety variables in terms of basic principles involved. The dichotomies are: (a) *Characteristic* versus current (trait versus state), (b) *overall* versus *specific* and (c) *existent* versus *proneness*. This kind of a scheme provides a better understanding of the variables that need to be included in the anxiety assessment instruments. Further, it will help to increasingly focus on specific identifiable variables, in the measurement of anxiety.

Epstein's Integrative Model

Epstein (1972) presented a model to describe basic

anxiety which is an unpleasant state of high diffuse arousal. Three explanatory concepts are proposed namely *primary over stimulation, cognitive incongruity* and *response unavailability*. Fundamentally, distinctions are made among fear, anxiety and arousal. Fear is an avoidance motive, and arousal is a reaction to all sources of inner and outer stimulation. Arousal encompasses fear and anxiety as well as other positive and negative motives and emotions. Anxiety is defined, as a state of diffuse arousal, following perception of threat or an unresolved fear. A set of basic propositions on the nature of arousal are presented. It is argued that organism in order to survive must defend itself against excessive stimulation and be responsive to lesser amount of stimulation. The arousal system has something to do with the development and expansion of awareness. At low levels, an orderly expansion of awareness occurs. In contrast at high levels there is defensiveness against stimulation (which is experienced as aversive). The present information is not adequate to deal with all the parameters that influence the relationship between expectancy and reactivity.

Anxiety research though extensive has somehow neglected important issues concerning young children. As a result of this, scientific planning and understanding of the need for child welfare programmes in our country has remained more or less a trial and error attempt, not even touching the fringe of the problem. With the rapid social and economic change and the shifting composition of the population towards younger age the Indian family and the child growing in it are exposed to many stresses and strains. The effect of these pressures on the child is seen in the child's failure to adjust to his surroundings and prevalence of a wide variety of behavioural problems. The present research is an attempt to dig into the immediate family environment through appropriate techniques and identify the crucial antecedent variables as well as to examine the nature of behavioural difficulties experienced by the child as a result of such adverse effects. In this, the present attempt may be considered to fill the lacuna of inadequate information about the growing child's emotional and behavioural problems with special reference to anxiety.

2

Review of Literature

The available literature on anxiety in children is reviewed in this chapter by selecting and arranging the reported studies under the following three sections :

1. Tools for measurement of anxiety in children,
2. Studies on anxiety in children in relation to antecedent variables, and
3. Studies on anxiety in children in relation to consequent behaviour correlates.

Tools for Measurement of Anxiety in Children

Measurement of anxiety in children is more or less identical to the methodology of measurement in adults. The only difference noticeable is the lack of adequate data regarding the psychometric characteristics. Ruebush (1963) speaks of *two* major categories of tools and techniques of measurement of anxiety in children. First, techniques which measure anxiety as *state* variable, included in which are, questionnaires, projective techniques and verbal analysis techniques. It is to be noted that there are questionnaires available, which measure anxiety as a trait variable also (Cattell Schierer, 1961). Second type of tools are those procedures which approach anxiety as a *process* variable. There are a variety of procedures developed for experimental manipulation of the stimulus conditions and techniques of recording relevant physiological measures.

In this review, main emphasis is on the measurement of anxiety as a state or trait variable, hence we will not be dealing with the second category of procedures. Therefore what follows in the pages is a discussion of various tools for measurement of anxiety in children as a state and/or trait variable.

Tools which view Anxiety as a State Variable

Questionnaires

Children's Manifest Anxiety Scale (CMAS). Castaneda, McCandless and Palermo in the year 1956 developed the CMAS for use with groups of children. This is an adaptation (through modification in working, format and instructions) of the Taylor's Manifest Anxiety Scale (TMAS). The CMAS consists of 42 items in English judged to be most appropriate for children. In addition, there are 11 items to constitute what is called L-scale. This particular L-scale is Intended to measure a child's tendency to consciously censor or to falsify responses to the anxiety items. Therefore, subjects scoring very high L-scale scores have to be excluded from further consideration.

The definition of anxiety as used by the test authors is that it is a diffuse and chronic condition of psychological and somatic tension, restlessness, distractibility, fatigue, irritability and predisposition to anxiety attacks on slightest provocation. Therefore by definition, CMAS is a measure of child's tendency to experience a general and chronic state of anxiety rather than to experience anxiety in a specific situations or as a process or transitory phenomenon.

The reliabilities of CMAS reported are in the range of .85 to .90 (Castaneda, 1956; Finch, 1974; Hollowy, 1961; Horrowitz, 1962; Kitano, 1960; Palermo, 1959).

The validity of CMAS is somewhat paradoxical because of the contradictory research evidence concerning the measure of clinical anxiety supposed to be tapped by this scale. Ruebush (1963) presents a review of number of studies on this point.

Extensive normative data is available for CMAS (Castaneda, 1956; Hollowy, 1961; Keller Rowley, 1962; Palermo, 1959). This scale is used with elementary school children at all grade levels above the second grade. Some studies report no grade difference (Castaneda, 1956; Keller Rowley, 1962), but other studies found inverse relationship between grade levels and CMAS scores (Morgan, Smith Rosenberg, 1960; and Palermo, 1957). Evidence concerning sex differences is equivocal with some studies reporting that girls obtain significantly higher scores than boys (Castaneda 1956; Palermo, 1957; Rosenblum, 1958), whereas others found no sex differences (Hollowy, 1961; Keller s Rowley, 1962).

Though sporadic attempts have been made to adapt CMAS to vernacular language in our country (Muralidharan, 1971; Sandeep, 1975) normative data on India children is not made available.

The General Anxiety Scale for Childern (GASC)

This tool was developed by Prof S.B. Sarason, K.S. Davidson, F.F. Lighthall, R.R. Waite and B.K. Ruebush at Yale University in the year 1960. The GASC measures general anxiety which could be used to find out or measure the relationship between anxiety in a specific situation (tests) and also anxiety in a variety of other situations. Designed as a tool to measure general anxiety, GASC is used within psychoanalytical framework. The scale has adequate reliability but the validities are low and yet statistically significant. The items were selected in such a fashion that they were consistent with Freud's definition of anxiety. The GASC contains 34 items concerning anxiety about a number of situations like: "If you were to climb a ladder, would you worry about falling off ?"; "Do you get a funny feeling when you see blood?" etc. The GASC items were found to be internally consistent but the scores have a tendency to decrease after a period of varying intervals, (Nijhawan, 1972; Sarason, 1960). Cox (1959) reported the test validity in the range of .03 to .34. The values of reliability reported by Nijhawan (1972) are .84 (splithalf) and .85 (K-R).

Normative data is available for American, English and Australian School children (Cox, 1959; Saranoff *et al.*, 1958). Normative data for Indian children are not available.

The Test Anxiety Scale for Children (TASC)

The TASC was developed by Sarason, Davidson, Lightall, and Waite (1958). The TASC is identical in its format and method of administration to the general Anxiety Scale for Children (GASC). TASC is a measure of physiological concomitants and subjective experiences of anxiety in a specific class of situations rather than in a variety of different situations. It consists of 30 items about evaluative test-like situations and subjective experiences of anxiety in such specific class of situations. The items were selected to be consistent with Freud's definition of anxiety, e.g. "Do you worry when the teacher says that she is going to ask you questions to find how much you know?", "Are you afraid of school tests?".

The test is used successfully with high school population. Studies report, the test is internally consistent and reliable (Cox, 1959; Nijhawan, 1972; Sarason, 1958, 1960).

Normative data is available for American, English, Australian and Norwegian elementary school children and also for a high school version of the scale. This test measures only a child's anxiety in test like situations, and therefore is used to measure the child's proneness to experience anxiety while taking a test. Generally the two scales TASC and GASC are to be conjointly administered.

Cattell's questionnaire measurement of trait anxiety in children (QMTAC) : Cattell's QMTAC (1963) is assembled from the High School Fersonality Questionnaire (Cattell, Beloff a Coan, 1958). The latter is appropriate for children between 11-18 years of age and is available in two equivalent forms, and yields scores on 14-first order personality factors (e.g., excitability, dominance) and on several second order factors, one of which is defined as clinical anxiety. The QMTAC is a specific measure of this second-order anxiety factor in children. It consists of a battery of 50 items, covering several anxiety-related primary factors. A separate questionnaire for the younger age group (below 11 years) is not available. Little is known about normative data and the psychometric characteristics of the test on Indian children.

Defensiveness scale for children (DSC) : Defensiveness scale for children (DSC) was developed as a measure of defensiveness to be used in conjunction with TASC (Davidson Sarason, 1961). It is composed of 11 lie-scale items (e.g. Has any body ever been able to scare you ?) which was previously included in GASC, plus three items to pick up negative response set (e.g., Do you like to play in the snow ?) plus 24 items designed to measure the tendency to deny the experience of negative feelings such as anxiety, guilt, hostility and inadequacy even when their expression is appropriate (e.g. Are there some people that you do not like ?). Ruebush (1963) reported a high split half reliability of the scale (.82). Though it was developed recently the initial studies about its validity are promising. There is evidence that conflicts experienced by defensive children are manifested more directly (Ruebush, 1961).

Some Novel Approaches to the Measurement of Anxiety in Children

In addition to the above, there are some innovative methodologies developed for the measurement of anxiety in children. Let us review a few such devices to illustrate the new trends,

Heath (1965) has designed phrase association test (PT) for the purpose of determining an individuals' anxiety thresholds for given interpersonal areas. Test stimuli are 48 five word phrases (e.g., He suddenly struck his father) representing six interpersonal threat areas (e.g., Rejection by mother) as well as neutral content. The subject responds by giving the first word or sentence that comes to his mind, and responses are scored in terms of specific criteria (e.g., Reaction time, Repetition of a stimulus word). Scoring reliability and split half reliability are both very high (.90). The construct validity for the PT is evidenced by investigators who have used the test. One snag in this test is that it requires considerable language ability and hence its use with lower age groups is doubtful.

Another novel approach to assess anxiety is the Anxiety Differential (AD) developed by Alexander and Husek (1962). This is intended to measure current anxiety in given areas (e.g., the anxiety present just prior to an examination). It is based on the assumption that a person who is anxious for a short period perceives thinks differently from when he is not anxious. The test is modeled after the semantic differential technique and consists of a series of parrings-some quite novel of scales and concepts (e.g. FINGERS; Stiff-relaxed). The anxiety side is determined empirically. Preliminary reliability and validity data are impressive. This test also requires linguistic skill, which precludes from considering its use with young children.

Still another approach to the assessment of anxiety is the one developed by McReynolds (1958). *It is called incongruency technique*. The procedure is based on McReynolds' theory of anxiety which holds anxiety to be a function of unassimilated affecto-cognitive material. Percepts are assumed to be unassimilable when there are signicant incongruencies in the region of the cognitive structure into which they would be incorporated. The technique attempts to identify such areas of incongruency. The preliminary findings are encouraging. However, empirical support for this technique is not available.

Other psychometric techniques which may be mentioned here, are the two objective measures developed by Cattell and Schierer (1960). The items are not obviously related to anxiety, hence not likely to be answered by non anxious group. The two objective measures are: (a) eight parallel form of anxiety battery (1960). Inter form reliability is .41 to .85, (b) objective analytical anxiety battery by Cattell and Schierer (1965) consisting of ten subtests. These are not suitable for use with young children.

Projective Techniques

Measurement of anxiety through projective techniques does not seem to have generated much interest and also appreciable empirical support. Although theoretically speaking one would expect greater success with projective techniques, the reasons for lack of popularity may be attributed to the complex scoring procedures and superior interpretative skills. Now we will review a few often mentioned projective devices. Temple and Amen (1944), Dorkey and Amen (1947), Amen and Renison (1954) developed a projective technique for use with pre school children. It consists of a series of pictures of child's activities (e.g., child's eating) in which the face is a blank and the child has to choose for it a happy or unhappy face. The idea is clever but in practical use much support does not seem to have been secured. Further modifications are attempted with little or no significance.

Rosenblum and Callahan (1958) introduced a children's anxiety pictures test. This correlated negatively with CMAS. It is released for wider use in 1979 with supportive normative information. The newly released test consists of 40 black and white plates selected by item analysis. This test can be given either individually or in a group. Norms for 5 to 12 years are available based on a sample of 558 children, takes 10 minutes to administer and scoring can be mastered easily. It takes 5 to 10 minutes to score.

Verbal Analysis Techniques

It has been observed that evidence of current emotional disturbances show upon ones' spoken and written output as well. Dollard and Mowrer (1947) speak of discomfort relief Quotient (DRQ) which appears to be the first systematic attempt to measure tension through this channel. The DRQ is the ratio of the number of discomfort words to the number of discomfort plus relief words in given verbal samples. The available evidence on the efficacy of this technique is not highly encouraging though it is attractive for evaluating objectively changes following therapy. These verbal analysis techniques heavily involve content and hence may not be widely applicable.

Observer Rating Techniques

The use of observer rating techniques for assessing anxiety is sufficiently demonstrated in the literature. We can see some systematic attempts to develop standard rating procedures as early as 1949, Elizur (1949), made use of a 9 point rating scale with a high inter-rater reliability. This was followed by a number of others (Buss wiener, 1962; Durkee & Baer, 1955; Hamburg, 1958: Hamilton, 1959 and Raskin, 1962) who similarly developed rating procedures with reasonably high inter-rather reliability. McReynolds (1965) developed an anxiety behaviour check list which consisted of 25 behaviours typically true of anxiety. The inter-rater reliability for this device was .84. The simplicity of rating procedures makes observers ratings one of the most popular techniques. Particularly in clinical settings, ratings based on a combination of self reports and objective observation, must yield satisfactory measurements. However, the available empirical data is not sufficient to warrant such a conclusion.

Physiological Indices

The physiological indices of anxiety include electrical resistance of the skin, systolic and diastolic blood pressure, heart rate and so on. There is enough evidence to show a positive relationship between changes in such physiological measures and anxiety. The use of physiological indices involves instrumentation and technology which are often complex and difficult in every day situation. Perhaps they are most suitable in experimental studies where the effects of induced conditions are to be studied.

From the above survey of available tools we notice that ease of administration, scoring and interpretation are some of the important consideration in the choice of the tool. Further, the linguistic skill of the respondent poses special problems in the measurement of anxiety in children. There is always the possibility of the very nature of their procedures. Lawrence (1972) correlated some common approaches to measure anxiety. The correlations were not significant. Pichot and Debois (1973) discussing the methodological problems compared fourteen frequently used questionnaires, Say that the questionnaires with cumulative rating system are incompatible with multifactoral structure of anxiety and they stress on the fact that time factor over analysis must be considered. Bridges (1973) discussed the practical aspects of the use of psychological tests designed to measure anxiety, pointed that the association between TMAS with Eyscnck's personality inventory suggest either both relate to a general variety of emotional instability or they both measure the tendency to experience anxiety.

After reviewing all the merits and demerits of the various tools, it is found that questionnaires can be used more advantageously for research because of the ease of scoring and administration. This is the major advantage over projective techniques (where scoring and interpretation are combersome).

From the list of questionnaires reviewed in this chapter, it can be said that CMAS is a widely used tool because of its simplicity is content, format, administration and scoring. The TASC and GASC though used in research are not so extensively used as CMAS.

Studies on Anxiety in Children in Relation to Antecedent Variables

The term *antecedent variables* is used in the sense that they either contribute to the development of anxiety or may get associated with anxiety behaviour by anteceding the overt manifestation of anxiety in children. From this point of view, we can recognise two major groups of variables, namely the relevant demographic variables and family variables (e.g,, family structure, family environment). We will present a review of some of the relevant studies focussing on these two groups of variables.

Anxiety and Demographic Variables

Among the several demographic variables, the most frequently considered ones are age, sex and social class. It is needless to emphasize the psychological significance of these parameters in our discussion on anxiety behaviour in children. The meaning and implications of these parameters transcend the bounds of their were physical definition. It is particulary so because in view of the fact that these parameters have rich connotative significance to the inter-pretation of such complex behaviour as anxiety.

Age : In assesssing the influence of age two questions may be posed. Firstly, what is the earliest age at which children experience and overtly manifest anxiety which could be detected through a standard test ? Secondly, does anxiety increase with age ?

In the literature, there are a few studies which provide some evidence to show that anxiety (fear) could be seen in the responses to a set of pictures in a projective test as early as pre school years (Dorkey Amen 1947; Bauer, 1976; Temple s Amen, 1945).

Dorkey and Amen (1947) have further shown that anxiety responses increase with age (33.3%—3 Yrs., 10 mos group; 43.0%—5 Yrs, 8 mos group). Bauer (1976) examined, developmental changes in the structure of fears of kinder garten second and sixth grade children. For this purpose he chose 60 children belonging to 4-6 years, 6-8 years and 10-12 years. The interview method was used by giving a set of *three* unstructured questions :

> All of us are afraid of something, but we are afraid of somethings more than others. What are you afraid of most ? Some times we are afraid when we go to bed at night. Are you afraid when you go to bed ? What are you afraid of ? Tell me about it. Some times after we go to bed at night and have fallen asleep we have dreams. Some times dress scare me. Did a dream ever scare you ? Draw a picture and tell me about it.

These interviews were taped for content analysis. Analysis of interview content revealed decreases with grade level in the frequency of occurance of fears with imaginary themes such as fear of ghosts and monsters, of bed time fears and of frightening dreams, and an increase in the frequency of realistic fears involving bodily injury and physical danger. These findings suggested the presence of a developmental sequence in the structure of fears (from formless and imaginary to specific and realistic fears). The results are explained in terms of language acquisition, social expectations and sex roles. Though this study is not directly on anxiety behaviour, a likely parallel may exist with regard to anxiety manifestations.

Nobody has clearly tried to explain why anxiety should increase with age although it is logically and psychologically to be expected. It is well known that emotional responses are learnt, by interaction with one's environment and a range of such emotional responses naturally increase with more experience. Maturation and growth further add to the quality of expression of emotional responses. More studies are needed in this particular area, for clear cut evidence in favour of a positive relation between age and anxiety response in early years. The task becomes further complicated because of imprecise tools for assessment of anxiety in children particularly at the very young age.

With regard to age and anxiety response at higher age levels we have an equally unclear picture. Sarason (1960) found that thest anxiety increased with the age of children from first to sixth grade. Angelino, Dollin and Mech (1956) reported that when fears related to school situations were plotted against age, the general trend of the curves was somewhat negatively accelerated. Dutt (1968) found no significant change in anxiety scores in relation to age. Morris, Franklestein and Fischer (1976) found significant decrements in anxiety scores with increasing age. Nijhawan (1972) after testing 729 high school children reported that thest anxiety decreased with age.

One reason for such confusing state of affairs may be that the different investigators have used different conceptual definitions of anxiety. We know that the trait measure of anxiety and the state measure of anxiety may not give the same results therefore the general anxiety and test anxiety measures are likely to yield different results not necessarily indicating contradictory evidences.

Sex: Sex differences have been widely investigated. Angelino *et al.*, (1956) reported sex differences regarding fears and worries about safety, school, personal appearance and school relations among school children. Castaneda *et al.*, (1956) found no significant sex differences among children in anxiety scores.

Some studies report evidence for presence of sex differences in favour of girls (Bledsoe & Joseph, 1973; Davidson & Sarason, 1961; Muralidharan, 1971; Nijhawan, 1972; Sandeep, 1975) while others reported absence of such sex differences (Hollowy, 1961; Morris *et al.*, 1976 & Mulroy, 1968).

One possible source of explanation for the observed conflicting findings is differential parental attitudes and standards in bringing up boys and girls across different cultures.

Social Class Level (SCL): The term social class level refers to a combined effect of social placement, economic status and educational background of the parents of the particular family to which a child belongs. This social class is one of the most crucial variables which influences many psychological manifestations.

There is a diversity of opinion about the exact effect of social class on anxiety. Some studies report evidence in a definite support of social class effect on anxiety (Angelino *et al.*, 1956; Dale, 1968; Hawks Koff, 1970; Murolidharan, 1971), whereas Dutt (1968) found no significant effect of social class on anxiety scores in children.

Angelino *et al.*, (1956) found that ***boys*** of upper socio-economic group and ***girls*** of low socio-economic group reported more fears. Dale (1968) examined the relationship between anxiety and occupational class of parents of children. Administering a revised Boxall school anxiety test on 1,120 first year grammar school pupils in 42 schools reports that scores on anxiety are consistantly related to the occupational class. The most anxious pupils in his sample came from the lower social class. Hawkes and Koff (1970) present normative data on private and public elementary school children using a scale of general anxiety which had selected items from both the CMAS and the GASC. This general anxiety scale was administered to 211 children from upper middle class and 249 Negro children trom upper middle class and 249 Negro children from low socio-economic background. They reported significant statistical differences (representative of social class). Lower class children were found to be more anxious than middle class children. Among the lower class group, minority group seems to experience greater anxiety than other lower class group. Muralidharan (1971) found that girls from high socio-economic status group had more anxiety than boys of the same group and boys from low socio-economic status had higher anxiety scores than their counterparts.

Some investigations have reported evidence of high anxiety in low socio-economic groups (Nijhawan, 1972; Romey, 1976; Sandeep, 1975; Southworth, Albert & Gravath, 1974; Zilavner s Luz,.1974).

But Joel (1957) in a study comparing the American and English boys reported a tendency for low socio-economic group to exhibit least anxiety in both the samples. Murrell (1971) says that members of average families had better adjustment scores than higher or lower socio-economic groups. Sarason *et al.*, (1960) argued that correlation between social class and anxiety would be expected to be positive but small, since test anxiety may occur in a family even when least stress was given to academic achievement.

Though research on social class and anxiety has been done on a large scale it does not give a clear picture. The possible reason might be that the particular context in which the term social class has been used were not the same. Another way of assessing social class effect is by studying the effect of type of school on anxiety. It is true, that schools which charge high fees and managed by private agencies are preferred by parents of upper economic status whereas Municiple schools or schools directly administered by Government etc,, are preferred by parents of low socio-economic status. Children from the lowest economic status attend these schools in large numbers as the cost is low. It is generally believed that schools managed by private agencies exert more pressure on children for achievement and enforce strict discipline than do schools administered directly by Government and sided institutions. Therefore we may expect children studying in the private schools to score high on anxiety tests. Because of this possibility the type of school assumes importance in the analysis of antecedent factors. Let us look into the reported evidence on the type of school and anxiety.

We have four studies that report a positive relationship between anxiety and the type of school. Triffinger Ripple (1968) reported rank order correlations between teachers' ratings and pupils' score on anxiety scale was highest when teachers ranked the same sex pupils, lower when ranked the whole class and lowest when ranked by the opposite sex. This study advocates the importance of mixed schools. Another study by Dale (1968) also supported this finding. According to Dale (1968) pupils from single sex schools had slightly higher anxiety scores than pupils of mixed schools. Thomas (1970) found significant variability in both general anxiety scale as well as CMAS and types of school. Muralidharan (1971) reported significant differences on CMAS scores between schools charging higher rates of fee and schools charging lower rate of fees. High fee school girls were more anxious than others and low fee school boys were more anxious than girls of the same school. It provides additional support to the effect of social class on anxiety.

Nijhawan (1972) reported no significant effect of type of school on anxiety implying that the type of school had little effect on anxiety.

Once again the relationship between anxiety and social class is not definitive with reports of evidence both positive and negative or no relationships. Such a state of affairs can be attributed mostly to lack of properly conducted researches exclusively to investigate the problem. It is impossible to underscore both theoretically and practically the influence of social class on the overt emotional behaviour. Hence it is necessary to research more, this particular aspect.

Intra family Variables: Family plays a vital role in shaping a child's personality. The behaviour of a child is the resultant of a network of forces acting on him within the family as well as outside. The importance of family as a dynamic variable need not be over emphasized. Some relevant aspects that may be included under this area are family structure, quality of adjustment among members in the family, parental attitudes and family environment. Each of these variables contribute its mite to the development of a child's personality. There are some studies available on the effect of levels of adjustment of family members on family inter-action variables, levels of agreement among parents of normal and disturbed children, effect of different types of family structures and family tension on anxiety in children. These will be reviewed in the following pages.

Endsley (1976) reports that parents and dhildren of same sex tend to get mutually reinforced by identical behavioural characteristics. For example, ***fathers*** tend to like and encourage ***masculine*** behavioural characteristics in their ***sons***, similarly ***mothers*** tend to like and encourage ***feminine*** behavioural characteristics in their ***daughters***.

Byasee and Murrell (1975) tested whether parents of disturbed and autistic children exhibited more disagreement between themselves than parents of normal children. For this purpose they compared with parents of normal children with six parents of disturbed and autistic children each with unrevealed difficult task which yielded 4 measures of family interaction. They are spontaneous agreement, choice fulfilment, decision making time and index of normality. They confirmed the expectation that parents of autistic children disturbed children had more disagreement between themselves than the parents of normal children. This study throws light on the importance of parental agreement on emotional development in children. In other words there is a suggestion that disagreement may be an antecedent variable to emotional disturbance. Murrell (1971) compared 30 non clinic tetrads on two family interaction variables on the basis of social acceptance and achievement effort scores of their ten year old sons. Based on the scores, the families were divided into high adjustment, average adjustment and low adjustment groups. The major finding of this study is, that the members of average adjustment had high normality scores than corresponding members of high and low adjustment families. This lends additional support to the importance of family as a variable in explaining anxiety in children.

What is the role of family structure and tension in the development of anxiety? Previously reported evidence stresses on the need for harmony or adjustment in family life for normal emotional development. Lack of such harmony may cause emotional disturbances. But Nijhawan (1972) reported absence of significant difference between high anxious (HA) and low anxious (LA) children with reference to family structure (e.g. husband dominance, wife dominance etc.). The extent of disagreement between parents about the family activities was measured by the family questionnaire. It was found that high anxious boys report more tension between their parents than low anxious boys but similar evidence was not found in the case of girls. The investigator explained this finding in terms of a tendency among all to be more defensive than boys on family matters and identify themselves (among girls) with their parents more than boys do. A review of the studies on the effect of parental attitudes, conflict or disharmony on emotional development in children will follow immediately.

Parental attitudes : Parental attitudes on child rearing undoubtedly have definite effect on their children's behaviour. This is much more so because children spend much time with their parents particularly during the early years. One of the most frequently used device for assessing parental attitude is the Parental Attitude Research Instrument (PARI), developed by Schafer & Bell (1958). A detailed description of this tool is given in Chapter IV.

Studies on the relationship between parental attitudes and anxiety in children may be categorized into two major types. In the first type, are included studies which directly deal with the problem by comparing differences in the attitudes of parents of two groups of children such as emotionally disturbed versus normal children. In the second type are studies wherein disturbed parents themselves are compared with non-disturbed parents, *vis-a-vis* the interactions with their children.

There are three studies which come under first category which will be reviewed. Devereaux (1963) studied 131 boys and 123 girls on possible relationship of anxiety and need affiliation with only one question in the questionnaire. It read the boy/girl gets easily upset or worried. Children who received occasional spanking were on a low score in anxiety. Those who repeated frequent spanking or none at all scored high on anxiety showing that too rigid or too permissive attitudes leave the child in a mess. In another study by the same author (1961) it is found children who reported the parents as either high or low on expressive rejection and physical punishment rated high on anxiety and gang association. Nijhawan (1972) studied the attitudes of parents of 729 children by administering PARI. Subsequently 31 pairs of HA and LA children were studied with regard to parent-child relationships and early childhood experiences. Subjects falling above 15th percentile and below 25th percentile of the scores in TASC and GASC was the criterion used to identify HA and LA subjects. The main findings of this study may be summarized as follows:

More parents of HA children than LA children favour the statements from (Parent attitude scale) regarding parents' unquestionable authority over children, keeping children under strict discipline and beating the children for misconduct. They also believed that children should be helped in the little difficulties of life and that they should not hide anything from their parents. Mothers and fathers of HA children showed more discrepancy between their attitudes than those of LA children. Parents o HA children also gave more extreme answers than parents of LA children. Family interactions can be very powerful and produce emotional problems in children. In this context some of the interesting questions which arise are to mention a few. Are there genetic basis for levels of anxiety between parents and children? Is the anxious behaviour learned from parents through home and other interactional processes and so on. Towell (1977) after extensively reviewing some of the evidences in literature, examined, the anxiety levels between parents and children with a pilot study on 25 families selected at random from the families attending a Family Practice Centre at Spartanburg general hospital, in South Carolina. There were both black and white families in the sample (predominantly black families). Anxiety was assessed by State-Trait anxiety inventory (both children and adult forms). Based on the results obtained in the study Towell tentatively concludes that males in the family tend to move in the same direction of anxiety level (both state-trait) as do their mothers. Females in the family have a tendency to have scores negatively correlated with their mothers' scores; indicating they tend to more in the opposite direction of their mother's anxiety trait-level. At this paint there is insufficient data on fathers to make even a projection.

In another study, Perry and Millimet (1977), investigated the child rearing antecedents of high and low anxiety eighth grade children. The subjects were parents of 16 eighth grade children. First, the children were grouped as High Anxiety (HA) and low Anxiety (LA) on the basis of manifest anxiety defensiveness scale. Later the child was asked to take a block stacking task (22 blocks) once in the presence of father and once in the presence of mother. The order of presentation of the parents was randomized for all children. The parents were asked to estimate how many Blocks a child could stack while blind folded using the unpreferred hand. An idea of the average number of blocks a child could stack was given. The task was to stack as many blocks as posssible. The parent was asked to observe and help in any way except in the actual stacking process. The verbal interaction between parent and child was recorded on audiotape and later analyzed for content.

The child was asked to complete a form entitled, "Family life" (adapted from the Parent-Child Relationship Questionnare PCRQ developed by Harvey and Felkner). At the same time each parent independently completed a questionnaire called 'child rearing' (Adapted from the Hereford's parental interview and the Harvey and Felkner's PCRQ). The results have shown that the parents of LA children felt that the difficulties they experienced in child rearing were widespread, and present in all families. Whereas parents of HA children were not as likely to make this claim believing that their problems were unique neverthless. The LA child perceived his parents as disagreeing in their evaluation of him. The HA child is more likely to be a product of a broken home. The HA child believes that he gets along well with his mother unlike his LA counterpart. The families of HA child that have remained together are characterized by inconsistency, disagreement, criticism and lack of definition of family rules. Sarason *et al.*, (1960) have published a book based on six years of research on anxiety in children of elementary school age. This publication reports extensive studies on several aspects of anxiety which are of great interest to clinical and child psychologists and others in behavioural sciences. One of the hypotheses investigated by them of concern to our discussion is parental attitudes and behaviour as evaluated by interview procedures. Thirty two pairs of HA and LA children (matched on grade, sex and I.Q.) and their mothers and a few fathers of these children were interviewed and compared on their evaluations of their children on a chcek list. Some of the interesting findings are the mothers of HA children were more defensive, mothers of LA children tell more, are more spontaneous and are less dependant on the interviewer in discussing their children's experiences and personality. There is some indication in their results that mothers of LA girls tend to deal more fully than mothers of HA girls with emotional aspects of their daughters in school life. It follows from this, that the defensiveness is more of the nature of concious withholding or distorting type or greater restraint in describing their children (result of unconscious defence). Child rearing attitudes and practices of the parents of those children were also studied with a scale consisting of 38 items selected from PARI. It was found that HA girls' parents made more extreme ratings than the parents of LA girls while there was no difference at all between HA and LA boys' parents in this respect. Further to this, parents of HA boys disagreed more between themselves than die the parents of LA boys. These finding suggest that parents of HA children shows extreme and markedly different parental attitudes. It is doubtful in the absence of extensive cross cultural studies on wide range samples whether parents of all HA children would consistently fit into the above description.

Let us consider some important recent studies on parents themselves. MMPI characteristics of mothers of pre school children (emotionally disturbed, oblique behavioural problems) were studied by Friedman (1974). He reports that mothers of emotionally disturbed children had significantly higher scores on 5 clinical scales (Depression, psychopath deviate, psychasthenia, Schezophrenia and hypomania), Hussaini (1975) reports a study on the changes in child rearing attitudes of mothers of emotionally disturbed children. This was a project on family intervention programme in Michigan. A revised version on PARI was administered to

23 mothers, at the time of enrollment and subsequently at the end of the project period (two years). The investigator however failed to obtain significant change in the child rearing attitudes in the mothers. But it is interesting to note that mothers with low education and with greater number of children, tended to have both anxious and controlling attitudes.

Cohler, Grunnebaum, Weiss and Gallent (1976) compared mentally ill mothers with mentally well mothers. According to this study there was not much of a difference between the two groups of mothers with regard to their evaluation of importance of establishing a formal relationship with their children.

We have some cross cultural studies, which are noteworthy. Ramey and Campbell (1976) compared 28 low class black mothers with 34 white mothers of same age infants. Low class white mothers significantly differed from the general population, being more external in their perceived focus of control, more authoritarian and less hostile and rejecting and less democratic in their self description on PARI. This study indirectly highlights the role of parental attitudes and socio-economic status, which play an important role as antecedent variables to behaviour problems of children. The measurability and the relationship between the German and US mother's child rearing attitudes was investigated by Rapp (1967) parent attitude surveys from 124 Florida mothers were individually matched with translated surveys completed by 124 German mothers from Baden in Southwest Germany. Matching was near perfect on three categories, social class, age and number of children in the family.

Significant differences were found between the German and US complete samples on all five scores obtained. The US mothers demonstrated scores indicating less controlling attitudes than German mothers. These differences were maintained in 13 of 15 cross national comparable class comparisons.

The analysis within social class showed similar relationships in both samples. Upper and middle class scores were very-much the same within each national sample; however, the lower class demonstrated the most controlling and authoritarian attitudes within the respective cultures. Social classes in the US were found attitudinally less variables than those in Germany with respect to child rearing attitudes. The PAS scores of German and US mothers were further compared with the scores on PAS obtained by mother of problem and non-problem children in Shoben's original study (1949). German mothers' scores approximated with scores obtained by mothers of problem children and US mothers' scores approximated with scores obtained by mothers of non-problem children. It is possible that German mothers are more conservative and less permissive than US mothers hence the observed differences.

Another set of family antecedents, relevant to our review, is brith order and family size which are not so extensively studied. There are four studies which directly deal with the problem of the effects of birth order on anxiety in children. Out of them only one study has examined the effect of brith order and family size on anxiety. Out of these only one study has examined both birth order and family size effect. Bharathi and Venkatramaiah (1976) examined the effect of birth order and family size on anxiety in 150 randomly chosen children from elementary schools, in Tirupati town in Andhra Pradesh. Anxiety was measured by an adapted version of CMAS. The following are the salient findings of the study:

1. The first born child tends to be more anxious than later born children with certain exceptions. The last born child in a family of 4 or more children tends to be more anxious than the first born.

2. Restrictions of the size of the family to two or three children seems to be more advantageous to the last born.

This is understandable if we presume that parents bring up their first born children with greater concern and care than subsequent children. However, one might argue that they are less prepared and less experienced, and therefore might even provoke more anxiety in the first born. This can be resolved only by carefully conducted further research. The effect of birth order on anxiety was also studied by Bradley (1968), Jacobs (1969) and Singh (1972). The first born often meets the expectation of the teacher, is more suspectible to social pressure and is more sensitive to tension producing situation (Bradley, 1968). An anxiety measure was administered and no differences were found between the mean anxiety scores obtained for 60 first and only borns and 60 later borns (Jacobs, 1969). The mean anxiety scores of first born was significantly different from the middle born and later borns (Singh, 1972).

The evidences so far reviewed have one common feature is thus in that, this first borns are more anxious than the later borns. The parents of first born tend to bring up their children in a way and different from others. These parental attitudes and child rearing practices will change with brith of subsequent children in the family.

Studies on Anxiety in Relation to Consequent Behavioural Correlates

Anxiety as an intervening variable, is responsible for a broad spectrum of behavioural consequences. Considerable research data is available on the correlation between behavioural consequencies and measured anxiety. Research investigators have mainly used two types of strategies for correlating anxiety and behavioural changes. Extreme groups of subject scoring high and low on a test of anxiety were compared, on certain hypothesized behavioural measures. In another type of strategy anxiety was stimulated in the labortory and the immediate consequences on the behaviour were assessed. Both these types of investigations have shown a somewhat consistent picture of the effects of anxiety on behavioural parameters. We shall present a brief review of some of the selected important studies particularly those studies which have used children as subjects. Studies on the physiological correlates were excluded for obvious reasons, from the purview.

Intelligence

Small to moderate negative relationships have generally been obtained between measures of anxiety and scores on conventional intelligence tests (McCandless Castaneds, 1956; Ruebush, 1960; Sarason *et al.*, 1960) while a few studies have failed to show a negative relationship between CMAS scores and intelligence test scores (Kitano, 1960; Mandler & Sarason, 1952; Trent, 1957). Performance on Koh's block design test by HA and LA subjects was specifically compared by Mandler & Sarason (1952). They found that the mean scores on Koh's block design test for LA subjects was higher than the HA group. This suggests the inhibiting effect of anxiety on the performance requiring perceptual ability. In addition, these effects appear to be long-ranged that transitory and to increase with grade level (Lighthall, 1959; sarason *et al.*, 1960). It also appears that qualitative differences between intelligence tests (test like or game like) affect the relationship between anxiety and intelligence (Sarason *et al.*, 1960). Several studies have reported effect between anxiety and intelligence test performance (Feldhusen & Klausmeir, 1962; Kerrick, 1956; Sandeep, 1975; Ruebush, 1960). Sandeep (1975) reported that above average intelligent boys were more anxiety prone than girls.

Learning and Problem Solving Behaviour

There are quite a number of studies showing relationship between anxiety and learning and problem solving. Some studies have reported positive relationship between anxiety and learning. Leherissy (1973) reported higher levels of anxiety states were associated with the learning of more difficult material and high among the subject were found to make more errors on the difficult portion of the learning task than were low anxiety state subject. Taylor and Spence (1953) found that anxious children made more errors and required larger number of trails to reach the learning criterion. Some studies (Farber & Spence, 1953; Maltzman, Fox & Morrisett, 1954) have reported negative relationship between anxiety and learning. Ruebush (1960) provided some evidence on the relationship between anxiety and performance of children in a simple and complex learning situation. High anxiety children were found superior to the relaxed children (LA) in the simple learning situation. This relationship was reversed when complex learning situation was introduced. The effect of anxiety and disposition of children in problem solving task among 60, 3 graders was studied by Masser (1970). Anxiety was experimentally aroused by having the subjects fail on an intellectual task. The performance of the children on decision time and errors on "*match*" *to sample task*" was studied. He has reported that induced anxiety reduced longer decision times. This was found to interact with disposition (impulsive versus reflective) of the children. Thurner and Wein (1972) tested 34, 4th graders with *Kinder Angst* test and found experimentally that high degree of anxiety aroused by difficult items persisted and it hampered the performance on easier items.

Scholastic Achievement

There are quite a large number of studies reported in the literature on anxiety and scholastic/academic achievement. Investigating the effect of peer group acceptance and academic achievement in two groups of children which were designated as LA and HA. McCandless and Castaneda (1956) found that school achievement was negative correlates with CMAS series. Donald (1973) divided 317 children belonging to 8-13 years age group and found significant differences between levels of achievement obtained between acccpted and non-accepted groups. Significantly higher correlations were established for high anxious children between group acceptance and achievement than non-anxious children. This study shows that anxious children are prone to lower levels of achievement. Sinha (1974) found that manifest anxiety symptoms had a debilitating effect upon scholastic achievement. Vishnoi (1975) reported that anxiety plays an important role in pulling down the achievement, perhaps to a greater extent in the case of under achievers than the over achievers.

Anxiety in children increased child's inability to cope with increased demands at higher grades (Marcelle, 1974; Lavine, 1965) after extensively reviewing the literature concluded that anxiety and academic achievement are not related. Oner (1977) reported negative correlation between anxiety and achievement. His sample consisted of 160 sixth grade boys and girls. Anxiety was measured by TASC and GASC and achievement skill test was given to measure. It may be reasonable to state on the basis of the available evidence that anxiety does affect achievement of children in school. There is a consistant evidence in support of this inference. A careful analysis will further suggest that the relationship between anxiety and school performance is not necessarily linear. It is therefore true, that anxiety in milder forms has facilitatory influence on performance. It is also true that people who have same loading on the trait anxiety, may react quickly and show stronger respone to relevant stimuli. In order to delineate in greater depths the relationship between anxiety and school performance particularly at younger age groups, the available evidence is not adequate and more research is needed across different cultural settings.

Emotional Behaviour (Fears and Dreams)

One of the major consequences of anxiety seen in the behaviour of children is poor emotional adjustment. This, more often than not manifests in the experience of fears and dreams. Typical anxiety dreams in adults are well recorded and described. In the case of children studies on this particular aspect are not many. In the following pages some reported studies are reviewed. However it was not uncommon for psychologists and psychiatrists working with children to use dream experience to understand emotionality and its related problems. The central issue concerning anxiety and dreams as we can understand from the studies available is whether anxiety produces more dreams, i.e., whether high anxious children report more dreams of types which are different from the dreams reported by low anxious children ? Theoretically speaking arguments both for and against the above contention can be adduced. For example, covert anxiety may get transformed through dream work mechanisms and appear in the dreams in the form of relevant dream imagery. Alternatively it is also possible that anxiety may manifest through other behavioural modalities and hence dream experience may be completely devoid of such imagery reflecting anxiety. What is happening in this case is the problem is solved through overt manifestation without a need for the involvement of the defense by the dream system. *In such a case HA children are likely to report less dreams.* Let us examine some of the evidences in the light of above contentions.

Sarason (1971) found that HA children were more self depreciatory and less content with themselves than LA children. Mishra and Singh (1972) tested 158 undergraduates with Hindi version of Cattell and Schierer's anxiety questionnaire have shown that anxiety is definite psychological morbidity and is almost certain to have adverse effects generally on work, social and emotional adjustment of the individual and stress the importance of guidance and counselling.

Despert (1937) proposed a hypothesis that emotionally disturbed children have fewer dreams, as their imagination is supposed to have been affected. No empirical support is reported nor any attempts made to verify the speculation. Lippman (1962) reported that 46 per cent of all children dreamt frequently and only 10 per cent were aware but not able to recall. The dream he explains, is a result of an incident or unsolved problem remembered by the child. The anxious child therefore, may try to find solutions to his problems in the dream.

The study of Bauer (1976) on developmental changes in children's fears already reviewed earlier needs to be mentioned with special reference to the use of dream contents in analyzing children's fears. Both in terms of numbers and content categories a noticeable sequence was observed. The higher incidence of fears in older children was explained as due to availability of verbal system in the communication.

Gnapp (1956) holds the view that specific anxiety reactions related to school remains hidden and this defense structure has its roots in the home environment. It is true for an young child that home is the place which offers protection and all the defence structures will be built around home only. Schierer (1961) developed a fear survey schedule to compare fears and anxiety scores and obtained a positive correlation of .49 showing that anxious children had more number of fears which that anxious children had more of fears which is to be expected. Investigating the fears of children Rodrigue (1972) categorized 46 types of fears in general and 48 types of experienced fear with the help of fear schedule and interview among children. Zolowitz (1973) described two broad themes for childhood fears. They were (a) phobias and anxieties of expectations and (b) themes of violent death and grievious affliction. The research information is rather thin and the issues concerning anxiety and dreams still remained open.

Speech and Language Functions

It is a common experience that anxiety or tension affects perceptibly one's ability to communicate. A change in pitch, voice and or a lack of clarity may result due to emotional disturbances. Some times it may even result in a more disorganised language expression.

Speech functions : That emotions affect the quality of speech is well recorded. Various aspects of speech such as pitch, voice, rhythm and articulation have been examined. Recently acoustic analysis of speech sounds has been shown to have special diagnostic potential for detecting early changes due to emotional disorders. Most of the studies available have used adult subjects and information about children is virtually not available.

Knower (1941) has reported evidence that expressions of emotions are strongly associated with variations (experimentally manipulated) in tonal quality and sequential pattern of voice expression.

Brody (1943) has reported evidence that, sudden changes in timbre, inflections or monotony, the rate of speech, pitch, intensity and deviations in the use of words, all might be expressions of underlying conflicts.

Dittman, Wynne and Lymen (1961) examined the psychological significance of linguistic (juncture-dividing points in speech between clauses; stress-variations in loudness and pitch) and para linguistic (vocalizations, voice quality, voice set) phenomena in speech samples of interviews with patients and excerpts from radio programmes. It was found that linguistic phenomena had very little psychological significance, but could be coded reliably. In contrast, para linguistic phenomena was shown to have higher psychological significance with poor coding reliability.

Kramer (1963) found that a person's changing emotional state and relatively stable personality characteristics can be judged from non-verbal qualities of voice thereby showing the relationship between voice and emotional disturbances. Oswald (1965) has successfully demonstrated the diagnostic value of acoustic methods in psychiatry. The physical parameters of speech sounds are shown to have distinctly different values and pattern between psychiatry patients and normal subjects. This is a novel, not yet fully exploited objective approach in early diagnosis of emotional disturbances. Ramsay (1971) has described significant differences in a study on speech pattern and personality between extroverts and introverts in the length of silence between utterances. In general introverts used longer silence between sentences, and in the case of persons high on neuroticism, the difference was small and inconsistent. Lester (1976) has further demonstrated the usefulness of acoustic methods in the diagnosis of early malnutrition in infants. The cry sounds of 12 well nourished and 12 mal-nourished male infants were compared using behavioural and acoustic measures. The cry of malnourished infant had an initial longer sound, higher pitch lower amplitude more arrhythmia and a longer latency to the next cry sound than the cry of the wellnourished infant. The similarity between the cry of the malnourished infant and cry of the brain-damaged infant suggested that malnutrition may affect the regulatory function of the central nervous system. This hypothesis was supported by additional findings which showed that the abnormal cry patterns in the malnourished infants were associated with a low-level orienting response to a pure tone stimulus as measured by the magnitude of heart-rate deceleration.

The studies so far cited in this review have only demonstrated in general terms the relationship between emotions and speech functions. More specifically the question of how anxiety mediates in causing variations in speech functions has to be answered by direct investigations. In the absence of such direct evidence, it is presumable that anxiety does produce measurable changes in speech functions.

Language functions **:** Language has two major functions in human interactions. Firstly, it allows us to communicate with one another. Next, it provides a system of symbols and rules which facilitate the thinking process. A symbol is understood as anything that stands for or refers to something other than itself. Words in any language are important components of symbol system. Psychologists have successfully demonstrated the value of the study of language in order to understand both the acquisition of language and the function of such a system in human communication. Myklebust (1970) considers language as symbol making behaviour. This definition of language lends itself to systematic procedures of behavioural analysis.

Noam Chomsky (1972) of Massachusetta Institute of Technology, U.S.A. has worked out generative models of language which have great significance in the field of psycholinguistics. Further the study of language structure and functions has enlarged our understanding of the relationship between brain and behaviour. In a language system, speech sounds are related to meaning, according to a set of rules. It is assumed that there are universal transformational rules which specify the steps by which such relations between sounds and meanings can be achieved. Not withstanding this, the development of language itself takes place in a predictable sequence, irrespective of cultural and linguistic differences. Logically therefore, it is relevant to consider the variations in the use of language as influenced by emotional states. One profitable area is to study the functions of the language in relation to emotions at early years of childhood. The reason being that it is the most sensitive area in cognitive development to the impact of emotions and the changes are easily detectable. In the present review, it is proposed to focus on certain typical tools in the assessment of language functions as well as empirical investigations which throw some light on the possible effects of emotional disturbances on the language functions particularly in children.

Tools for Assessment of Language Behaviour in Children

According to Perkins (1971) three basic types of language abilities namely, vocabulary, grammar and the functional use of language become of the central focus in the assessment of language behaviour. Each one of these basic t ypes of language abilities can be formally assessed through standard tests developed for the purpose. Anastasi (1972) gives a review of some of the tests. To assess vocabulary the frequently used tests are Dun's full range picture vocabulary test, per body picture vocabulary test.

There are several tests to measure comprehension and expression. The best known among them is the Illinois Test of Psycholinguistic Abilities.

One of the most carefully constructed tests to measure comprehension is the Illinois Test of Psycholinguistic Abilities (ITPA). This is an individual test for children between 2 to 10 years. In its design the ITPA follows the three dimensional model or a cube which is a condensed adaptation of C.B. Osgood's theoretical models of the communication process (Kirk and Kirk, 1971).

Channels	:	Auditory-Vocal Visual-motor
Processes	:	Receptive (understanding words and pictures) organizing (association of past and present inputs and education of relations) Expressive (expressing ideas in words or gestures)
Levels	:	Representational (Utilising measuring of linguistic symbols). Automatic (Utilizing habitual integrated patterns e.g., speed of perception, Role learning memory span).

The abilities covered by the ITPA are located at the intersections of the three dimension. For example, in the manual expression test (visual motor channel) expressive process, representational level, the child performs manual gestures to "show what we do with" each pictured object such as pencil sharpener, telephone and clarinet. In the grammatic closure thest (auditory vocal channel, Organising process, automatic level) the task is to complete oral statements such as "Here is a child. Here are three————", while shown the appropriate pictures. The entire battery consists of 10 regular subtests, plus two optional subtests.

Both the pictorial and verbal items of ITPA appear to be heavily loaded with culturally restricted content. The normative samples were drawn largely from middle class populations in five midwestern cities. For these reasons, the applicability of ITPA to children from lower socioeconomic levels and minority groups needs to be more fully ascertained. The test authors recommend the use of supplementary local norms.

For children who can write the picture story language test by Myklebust (1965) is another useful test. This test measures language productivity, syntactic correctness, abstractness or concreteness of meaning.

The test is applicable to children of age range 7 years to 18 years. The major objective in designing the picture story language test was to serve as a tool in the study of language developmentally and diagnostically. The test consisted of a 10 1/2" × 13 1/2" picture projecting a play situation about which the child is instructed to construct a story. The aspects of language measured by the study are productivity, correctness and meaning.

Productivity means amount of language expressed under given conditions referred as length unless an expression is of minimum length effective communication is precluded. An adequate number of words is essential as a pre-requisite for useful communication. This is measured in three ways by this picture story language test by ascertaining the total

3. To determine the achievement level of a given class in order to assess the progress made with in a year,

4. To compare the advantages of different educational methods,

5. To study the range and nature of written language abilities geographically,

6. To ascertain levels of written language ability for the purpose of grouping and teaching,

7. To define the errors of written language which characterize the performance of the deaf, aphasic mentally retarded, speech defective and emotionally disturbed,

8. To obtain data for comparatively analysing facility with the spoken, read and written word,

9. As a tool for studying grammar and the syntactical development of sentence structure,

10. As a measure of geometric deterioration of verbal behaviour,

11. As a measure of comparing language as used in various countries psycholinguistically, and

12. As an indication of literacy.

This test is attractive because of its simplicity in administration and well designed scoring procedures with adequate normative information. It is surprising that this test is not exploited in our country in the study of language behaviour. It is to be noted that this test is not suitable if one is merely interested in the speech and language development. However it has undoubted value in the diagnosis of speech and language pathologies.

Language development *per/se* can be assessed by a variety of tools available. To mention a few Vineland social maturity scale, Gessell's developmental schedules, Bayley's scales of infant development, piagetian scales. In addition to these, there are a number of special diagnostic tests, available for clinical evaluation of language disorders. Unfortunately, cross cultural, normative and psychometric characteristics of these tests are so inadequate as to make a proper evaluation of their universal application across different languages. Brown, Cazden and Bellugi (1962) with the help of speech samples of 12 Negro children, during play situations, reported that, the child's grammatical knowledge of language during I to III grades depends on the modelling and the frequency of approval and disapproval by parents. This study stresses the importance of modelling and reinforcement by parents.

Mehrebian (1970), tested language development on 127 children of all socio-economic status where age between 2 1/2 and 5 years using the following measures :

1. Picture vocabulary
2. Comprehension of simple commands
3. Comprehension of meaningless commands
4. Infliction
5. Judgement of grammaticalness of sentences and phrases.
6. Verbal imitation given in the same order.

Factor analysis of all these scales yielded one verbal ability factor which included all the six measures. The effect of anxiety on perceptual reading pattern of word phrases was studied by Titsworth and Amble (1973). In their study; 57 male and 57 female 5th and 6th grade children were given a phrase reading test and an anxiety test. It was found that high anxiety significantly limited the perception particularly among 3, 4 and 5 word length phrases. Bloom, Light, Brown and Hood (1975) studied four first born children of college educated parents over a period of 9 months at five intervals. The subjects' age at the beginning of the experiment ranged from 19 months and five weeks to 20 months and one week. The objective was to discover categories of semantic and syntactic relations between the earliest multiword utterances in children. The results have shown that the child's language structure is more adult like grammar and it contains both analytic and synthatic features of language in general.

Overview

The following salient observations could be made from a critical review of the literature presented in the preceding pages.

1. In the definition of anxiety and choice of appropriate tool there is no uniformity or consistency among different investigators. This has resulted in inconsistent findings.

2. Most investigations in the area of anxiety research have used adult human subjects. There are only a handful of studies on young children as a result of which generalizations regarding the effects of anxiety on the behaviour become questionable. More research on early childhood years, are particularly needed for scientific prognosis of adult mental health.

3. The role and involvement of age, sex and social class variables are not yet clearly understood in the face of confusing evidence in the literature. No doubt they are important, but clearly established trends are conspicuously absent. Generalisations are naturally difficult as cultural variations signifi-

cantly contribute to their meaning and interpretations.

4. The exact nature of family antecedent variables possibly involved in anxiety is not yet clear. It is so, even with regard to parental attitudes. Considerable theoretical basis exists in support of such family antecedents and parental attitudes playing a very crucial role. Once again cross cultural variation is a rule rather than an exception. More empirical investigations are needed to build up a strong evidence and a basis for planning effective intervention programmes in different societies.

5. The consequent behavioural changes strongly associated with anxiety are perhaps better delineated in the available researches. However, there is a demonstrated adult bias in the sample of subjects; certain relevant behavioural consequences like dream experience, creativity and human communication seem to have been neglected. The importance of examining the effect of anxiety as on such behavioural consequences need hardly any emphasis.

In the formulation of the problem of the present thesis and the development of hypotheses for research, the above observations served as the main source of the critical background. Our main concern in definition, selection and procedural details regarding the depedant variables was the investigation of the effects of anxiety in early childhood years. It is expected that such a concern and focus of interest is *need-based* with special reference to our country which has nearly one sixth of the world population of children below nine years i.e., 83 million children (Population Guidance Bureau, Washington, 1979).

3

Statement of the Problem and Hypotheses

Justification

The problem of anxiety in the psychological and related literature is well defined and perhaps most thorougly investigated. A review of the current conceptions of anxiety and the reported empirical studies in the literature, suggests the need for further probe into the antecedent and relevant consequent behavioural correlates particularly in early childhood. Cross cultural studies and much needed information to develop a broad based understanding of the manifestation of anxiety behaviour.

Now that the tools and techniques of the measurement of anxiety have been satisfactorily refined and conceptually strengthened, what is needed is perhaps data across different social backgrounds and cultural settings.

Studies on the problem of anxiety behaviour to fulfil the above stated needs in our country are negligibly few and inadequate. We need data and information with regard to possible influences, the parental attitudes, family structure and intra-family dynamics have, on the behavioural manifestations of anxiety in children, to device and develop effective preventive programmes in child care and allied services. In addition to this, the information available on the patterns of consequent effects of anxiety in children are not only inadequate, but often lack in quality. This *lacuna* is a major hurdle in the practical management of children both at home and in schools. It is not surprising if parents and teachers are not aware of the fact that certain behaviours are caused by anxiety but are either neglected or wrongly attributed to some other source.

Clinical psychologists, child development specialists and counsellors working with parents and teachers often have to work through such problems in the routine management of behavioural problems. A well designed and executed research study into these aspects is therefore expected to provide the necessary basic information which will further help in, implementing preventive intervention programmes.

The Problem

The problem of the thesis may be stated as a study of certain selected antecedent and consequent behavioural correlates of measured anxiety levels in a sample of elementary school children between 5 and 7 years. The scope of the investigation was confined to assess qualitatively and quantitatively the main and interactional effects of demographic and structure, on anxiety levels measured by a standard instrument. The consequent behavioural correlates selected are the *dream experience, speach and language functions,* which are evaluated by suitable tools and producers.

The main concern of the thesis was to gather scientific evidence on these parameters and examine them in the light of specific hypothesis framed.

Statement of the Hypothesis

The following hypothesis were set up for empirical verification, based on the review of existent literature reviewed in the previous chapter.

Hypotheses Related to Antecedent Variables

1.0 The effects of demographic and social class variables on measured anxiety in children are insignificant. In a multivariate analysis (three way analysis of variance) where sex, age and social class are treated as independent variables and anxiety as dependent variables, the results should indicate the following :

1.1 The main effect due to age is not significant.

1.2 The main effect due to sex is not significant.

1.3 The main effect due to social class is not significant.

1.4 The triple interaction is not significant.

2.0 The intrafamilial structure and dynamics constitute a major antecedent variable in the manifestation of anxiety behaviour in children.

2.1 There is significant association between measured anxiety levels and family structure as measured by the family structure and tension balance questionnaire.

2.2 The mean index of family tension balance as measured by the family structure and tension balance questionnaire differs significantly between HA and LA children.

3.0 Parental attitude is an important antecedent determinant of anxiety.

3.1 Parents of HA children tend to be relatively more dominant and authoritative than the parents of LA children.

3.2 Parents of LA childern are relatively more democratic than parents of HA children.

3.3 Parents of HA children score high on strictness, intrusion of activity and seggregation than parents of LA children.

3.4 Parents of HA children report relatively more marital conflict than parents of LA children.

3.5 The second order factors derived from the primary 23 scales reveal significant differences in the factor profile between the parents of HA aud LA children.

Hypothesis Concerning Consequent Variables

4.0 Anxiety affects the content and frequency of dream experiance.

4.1 HA children tend to experience and recall greater number of fear arousing dreams than LA children.

5.0 Anxiety has a disturbing influence on the speech functions of a child.

5.1 The mean pooled ratings (pooled from independent ratings by experts) of the pitch of the speech sample of HA children is significantly higher than that of LA children.

5.2 The voice quality of HA children is relatively poor than that of LA children as indicated by the mean ratings pooled from three independent raters.

5.3 The mean pooled ratings on the parameters of fluency of HA children is relatively lower than that of LA children.

5.4 The speech sample of HA children contains relatively more articulatory errors than the LA children.

6.0 Anxiety affects the use of communications through spoken language in children.

Communication through spoken language is analysed on the model of Myklebust's scheme, for written language.

6.1 The total words in the speech sample of LA children is significantly greater than the total number of words in a comparable speech sample of HA children.

6.2 The words per sentence in the speech sample of LA children is significantly higher than the words sentence of speech sample of HA children.

6.3 The syntax quotient computed for the speech samples of LA children is significantly higher than for the speech sample of HA children.

The specification and the choice of the exact procedure and statistical treatment of the data are made to highlight the main and intergraction effects of the antecedent and consequent variables on the dependent variable in question. The details of methodology tools and the quantitative procedures employed are described in the next chapter.

4

Method and Procedure

General Plan

The major aim of the study is to understand anxiety behaviour in children, in terms of certain antecedent and consequent behavioural correlates. For this purpose, the study is planned in two stages. First stage is preliminary evaluation of the major tools and the procedure to be finally employed. The second stage concerns the collections of primary data on a selected sample of children according to the standard procedure and design of study.

A sample of children in three age groups, (5, 6 and 7 years) is to be selected from a population of children attending elementary schools in the town of Tirupati, Andhra Pradesh. It is preferable to have equal number of boys and girls to facilitate easy statistical analysis of the data.

The antecedent and consequent variables are selected and defined on the basis of research information available for further probe. In addition to the usual age, sex and social class, two major antecedent variables namely family structure and dynamics; and parental attitudes are selected. The anxiety itself is to be measured using an appropriate test such as the Children's Manifest Anxiety Scale (CMAS). The major consequent variables are dream experiences, speech and language functions.

In the first stage of the study, the preliminary studies for the evaluation of the suitability of the tools, for the measurement of the antecedent and consequent variables are worked out.

In the second stage the primary data on both the antecedent and consequent variables are obtained on a sample of children. A measure of anxiety is also obtained.

It is planned to compare the antecedent and consequent variables between two groups of subjects who would be designated as high anxiety and low anxiety subjects using a standard criterion. Such a comparison is expected to reveal significant information as to the possible sources and manifestation of anxiety behavioural in children.

Subjects for Preliminary Study

The subjects for the preliminary study were 150 boys and girls studying in the I, II and III grades of elementary schools* in Tirupati town. There were 75 boys and 75 girls. They belong to three age levels namely 5+, 6+ and 7+ years. At each age level the sample had 25 boys and 25 girls, (25 × 2 × 3 = 150).

* Elementary school or primary school in the existing pattern of education in India gives instruction to children in the age groups 5+ to 12+ years. The first regular schooling begins at 5+ age in the first grade. The terminal grade for elementary education is the seventh grade.

Final Study

Three hundred boys and girls constituted the sample of subjects for the final study. There were altogether 150 boys and girls in the sample. These subjects were all students of I, II and III grades of elementary schools in Tirupati town and were 5+, 6+ and 7+ years old. At each age level there were 100 children (50 × 2 × 3 = 300).

Tools and Materials of Research

The tools used in the present research study may be broadly put under four headings.

1. Tools for the assessment of anxiety.
2. Tools for the assessment of social class.
3. Tools for the assessment of antecedent variables.
4. Tools for the assessment of consequent variables.

Tools for the Assessment of Anxiety in Children.

Description of the Tool

The most appropriate instrument for measuring anxiety in children is the children's Manifest Anxiety Scale (CMAS) developed by McCandless, Castaneds and Palermo (1956). The original instrument is based on Taylor's Manifest Anxiety Scale and consist of 42 items. There are an additional 11 items constituting a L-scale. Each item is answered yes or no. The CMAS by definition is considered to be a measure of children's tendency to experience general and chronic state of anxiety rather than a tendency to experience anxiety only in specific situations or as a process or transitory phenomenon. It is used to measure the level of anxiety in (elementary school) children at all age levels above the second grade.

The adapted version adopted by the author of this study had 40 items and 10 items on L-scale in Telugu language. Each item elicits an answer yes or no.

Administration and Instruction

The test is given in an informal fashion to the *individual* child. After establishing sufficient rapport each question is asked one by one and the answer is recorded by the investigator.

After establishment of initial rapport, the investigator instructs the child as follows : "Look here, I will now say a sentence, Listen carefully. Tell me whether you have the same thing or not. If you have the same thing say *yes*. If you do not have, say *no*. Now be ready." The investigator goes through the entire list of items slowly and methodically, recording each time the child says *yes* or *no*.

Scoring

The responses are scored according to a prepared key. Each correct answer is given one point. There will be two sets of scores. The first set is a score on the L-scale and the other is on the anxiety scale. The maximum possible L-scale score is 10 and anxiety scale score is 40. A high score on L-scale indicates presence of motivational distortions and therefore invalidates the test protocol. A L-scale score of 6 and above is considered very high for any further consideration ; the decision being to reject the protocol. The anxiety scores ranges from 0-40. It is presumed the higher the score the greater is the degree of anxiety. Tool for the Assessment of Social Class (a demographic variable).

The social class variable is measured using the SES scale (urban) developed by Kuppuswamy (1962). The scale yields a weighted grouping of social class levels into five groups ; on a linear scale based on occupation, education and income of the parents.

Note : There are a number of other socio-economic status scales (urban) subsequently developed in our country. The investigator preferred Kuppuswamy's scale because of its simplicity and proved efficiency in his part of the country.

Tools for the Assesement of Antecedent Variables

Family Structure and Tension Balance Questinonaire (FS & TBQ)

Description : This Questionnaire consists of two parts (Part I & II). Part I, has 22 items which describe household activities. The items are questions which ask who die, what ? The response to each question is recorded by encircling one of the eight categories provided.

Part II consists of questions on similar activities and 22 items. Each item describes a household activity and has further two sections. First section describes who decides what ? and second section about the frequency of disagreement or agreement between the parents about the described activities. The responses of the child are marked on a three point scale. For the first part, the response categories are Morher, Father or Both. Second section has another set of three responce categories namely Often, Sometimes and Never.

1. Who decides as what time you have to get out of bed ? M F B

   How often do your parents disagree as to what time you ought to be up ? O S N

Note : The above questionnaire is an adapted version of children's interview schedule (Family questionnaire) used by Nijhawan (1972). This childred's interview schedule is based on the family questionnaire developed by Herbst (I952). In the form used by Nijhawan, the children's Interview schedule had two parts (Part I & II) with 31 items on each part. These two parts together give the type of family pattern and an index of tension balance. The adapted version in our study is almost identical with regard to items (except 9 items which were deleted), method of administration and scoring procedures. No effort was made to establish reliability and validity etc., for this tool. The efficiency of the tool was taken for granted on the basis of its face and content validity together with the encouraging results reported by Nijhawan (1972).

Administration

Part I and II are both administered to each child. The investigator reads out each item and the response given by the child is recorded by encircling the appropriate response category.

Instructions

After initial rapport the investigator instructs the child as follows for the Part I.

"Listen to me carefully. I will read out a list of activities one by one slowly. Listen carefully and tell *who did* the activity" The entire list of activities is read out one after another and responses are recorded.

The items of Part II of the Questionnaire are administered to the child in the similar fashion as in the case of part I. The following instructions are given.

"Now listen again. I will read out each activity. Tell me *who decides*? Is it your father? Is it your mother? or both?" The investigator reads out the second half of the time and asks the child again 'tell me whether your parents disagree?' The response is recorded as before.

Scoring

Each area of activity within the family, there are three possibilities with regard to acting and deciding about various matters namely :

Activity

1. Ha—Huspand does the activity by himself.
2. Wa—Wife does the activity by herself.
3. Ba—Both do it together.

Decision

1. Hd—Husband decides by himself.
2. Wd—Wife decides by herself.
3. Bd—Both decide together.

On the basis of who did and who decided about various household matters, percentage of each family pattern was determined for each child as follows.

1. Husband dominance—percentage of items on which Wahd+Bahd
2. Wife dominance—percentage of items on which Hawd+Bawd
3. Autonomic—percentage of items on which Hahd+Wawd

4. Syncratic cooperative—percentage of items on which Babd

5. Syncratic division of functions—percentage of items on which Habd+Wabd

The pattern on which the greatest percentage of items fell for a certain family was considered to be its family structure. The family tension index is calculated by determining the extent to which disagreement existed about the various family activities using the following classification.

T = parents disagree sometimes/often.

T_o = parents never disagree.

Tension index* (the percentage of areas in which tension occurs) is calculaled as follows :

$$\text{Tension index} = \frac{T}{N} \times 100$$

Where T = Total number of T's

N = Total number of items sampled

*Note : Nijhawan (1972) uses the term *tension balance* for the same experience also. Greater the value of index (percentage), higher is the tension between the parents.

Parental Attitude Research Instrument (PARI)

Description

The PARI measures parental attitude towards child rearing and family life. Parental attitude research instrument was developed by Schafer and Bell (1958) based on the original inventory designed by Shoben. This instrument consits of 115 items. Each item describes a specific child rearing practice generally adapted by parents. These items are conceptually grouped under 23 sub scales with five items under each sub scale. These sub scales are given specific names such as strictness, deification and so on. Response to each item is recorded by marking on a four point scale (e.g.

1 Children should be allowed to disagree with their parents if they feel their own ideas are better   A a d D

In this study a Telugu version of the PARI (115 items) was prepared for administration and was used on the parents of children in this sample. Further, this test was factor analyzed by the investigator. It is possible to construct factor profiles and make suitable inferences.

Administration

The test is administered to parents preferably both following the usual procedure. The instructions and procedures to be followed as per the recommendations of the original authors are reproduced.

If the respondent is found inadequate to answer the questionnaire by himself, or herself the investigator may record the response by going through the items one by one during an interview.

Scoring

Each item is scored by assigning a value +2, +1, —1 and —2 corresponding to the response strongly agree; mildly agree ; mildly disagree and strongly disagree. The score for an individual is the sum of the scores over all the five items in a sub scale. Each subject gets, thus 23 scores, corresponding to the 23 sub scales. The scores, therefore range from -10 to $+10$ $5 \times \pm 2 = \pm 10$). To avoid negative scores a constant values of +10 is added. Hence the final score will range between 0 and 20 for each sub scale. These numerical values are interpreted as expressing the degree of attitudes along the continum favourable—unfavourable qualifying each sub scale.

Tools for the Assessment of the Consequent Variables

Dream Check List

Description: Children's dreams are a potent source for understanding their emotional state. A quantitative index of the dream behaviour is considered extremely useful in assessing the consequent effects of emotional experiences such as anxiety, frustration etc. Usually, dreams are analyzed qualitatively to bring out the underlying dynamics. The approach adapted in the present study is somewhat different in that it is quantitative and normative and hence useful as a research tool. A check list method is selected.

The dream check list has 20 items which are simple statements of typical anxiety dreams dreamt by children (e.g., In my dreams I see wild animals).

Administration

The test is individually administered after taking the necessary precautions for test administration to small children. Each item is read out. The child is asked to *say* whether the items have occurred in his/her dream or not during the recent past.

Scoring

The score on the test is number of items claimed to have occurred in the dreams of the child. The score for a child therefore ranges from 0 to 20. A high score says more than 10 is interpreted as an index of emotional disturbances.

Speech and Language Functions

Description: The list of materials and equipment for the analysis of speech and language functions include: (a) a test picture, (b) medium sized portable transmains tape recorder, (c) cassettes (of good quality), (d) remote microphone:

(a) The test picture is an enlarged photograph of a scenario size 30 x 25 cms showing a number of play materials in the *back ground* and a child playing with some of the play materials in the *fore ground*. The test picture used in the present study was shot on the model of test picture used by Myklebust in the picture story language test (1970). The original procedure of Myklebust was developed to study the development and disorders of written language in children. We have modified those procedures to suit our purpose namely to study changes in spoken language in children.

(b) Tape recorder. This is a standard commercial brand (Murphy Model RQ409MS) medium sized battery powered portable tape recorder. The standard speed of recorder is 1 7/8" inches per second or 4.75 cms/second.

(c) Sony C60 good quality cassettes are used.

(d) Microphone. A remote microphone (unidirectional) is used.

Administration

After establishing initial rapport, the child is given the test picture and is requested to tell a story about the picture. The child's response is recorded simultaneously on the Cassette tape recorder.

It is necessary ro take precautions while recording, in the field to avoid distortions, extraneous noise and to maintain accuracy of the acoustical quality. It is recommended to maintain the level of recording constant and the distance between the microphone and the speaker constant. In location recording like a public place or building it is recommended to cover the microphone with a cloth to increase the fidelity.

Scoring

The taped speech sample is analyzed later in two parts. In the first part the speech functions are analyzed In the second part language functions are scored, according to a set of procedure.

Scoring a Speech Functions

The cassette is replayed and the speech sample is rated quantitatively using two point rated scale. The rating was done by three raters who were specialists in child development and also experienced teachers. The following aspects were scored namely *pitch, loudness,* and *voice, rhythm, fluency, articulatory errors, tension* and *breathing pattern during* speech. The pooled ratings pooled over three raters constitute a Quantitative measure of the various aspects of speech functions selected. Higher the value better is the quality free from possible emotional disturbances.

Scoring of Language Functions

The basic materials for scoring language functions is the transcripted speech sample. The scoring dimensions of language functions are same as that of Myklebust (1970). The following dimensions are scored according to the procedure recommended by Myklebust (1970).

1. Total words (TW)
2. Total sentences (TS)
3. Words per sentence (WPS)
4. Syntax quotient (SQ)

Procedure

Initial Study: The subjects for initial study were selected from a population of children attending elementary schools in Tirupati town. The procedure employed for the selection of sample was multistage systematic random sampling technique. First, the schools were selected. Out of 33 schools in Tirupati town 11 were selected so as to represent location, medium of instruction and type of school. In the next stage, children belonging to three age levels namely 5+, 6+ and 7+ years were selected. At each age level, boys and girls were equally represented. A total of 150 boys and girls thus constituted the initial sample. The subjects in the sample were administered the CMAS, family structure and tension balance questionnaire, dream check list and speech and language analysis test, according to the standard procedures described earlier. The testing session was split into two halves, each half lasting for about 30 to 45 minutes. In the first session CMAS and FS & TBQ were given. The second session which was conducted in the later half of the same day included DCL, and speech & language functions analysis. PARI was given to the mothers of these children, in, separate sessions by visiting their houses on prior appointment.

The data so obtained on each test was examined for the suitability of the items in terms of language difficulty and appropriateness etc. Wherever necessary the items were changed by substituting better items or rewording for clarity. Items found unsuitable were omitted. The usual psychometric constants for evaluating a test, like reliability, score distribution, characteristics etc., were also studied.

The split half reliability coefficients were computed for following tools:

1. CMAS
2. Dream check list

3. Family structure and tension balance Questionnaire (FS & TBQ).

Inter correlations were computed between CMAS, Dream check list and FS & TBQ. The test picture for speech language function analysis was also administered to these children to find out the efficacy of the procedure proposed to be employed in the final analysis. The story response was actually scored according to the procedure and the trends were reviewed to see whether they require any modification or revision. The initial study also provided an opportunity to review and improve the procedure of recording the story response. Further the experience was found extremely useful in employing better methods of handling children during the testing sessions by avoiding the common errors. Essentially the experience helped the investigator to learn better problem solving techniques in working with small children and their parents.

Final Study

Selection of sample: The procedure employed for the selection of sample for the final study was identical to the procedure for the selection of initial sample. Using multistage systematic random sampling procedure, 300 boys and girls were selected from the same population of schools. However, the subjects in the final sample were totally new, that is to say none of the children in the initial sample was allowed into the final sample.

Procedure for Collection of Data

The major tools described earlier were all aministered to each child in the final sample according to the procedure for each tool already described. The administration of the tools was planned in three sessions. In the first session, the child was given CMAS and FS & TBQ. In the second session, Dream Check List and test for speech and language functions.

were given. The second session was usually held on same day in the afternoon. The third session was with mothers of these children. The investigator visited the homes of these children and interviewed their mothers for obtaining data on PARI. The visits were made generally in the evening by prior appointment.

Procedure for the Analysis Data

Qualitative Analysis : The primary data was subjected to both qualitative and quantitative analysis. Qualitative analysis was confined to comparisons of profiles of mothers on PARI facrors. Comparisons of ratings on various aspects of speech functions were made. Similarly the scores of language functions were also tabulated and examined. Graphic representation of age and sex trends in respect of CMAS scores was also restored to.

Quantitative Analysis: The quantitative analysis of data was confined to the application of the analysis of variance of data, on the major demographic variables to evaluate the main and interaction effects; testing of hypotheses using the chi square test and 't' test in respect of the effect of anxiety on the consequent behavioural correlates.

The PABI sub scales were factor analysed using the principle component analysis on IBM 360 computer. Varimax solution for the factor matrix was obtained. The nature and composition of factors were critically studied. The pattern of factors, loading in respect of children, high end low in anxiety were examined.

The qnantitative sources of PS & TBQ were evaluated testing the significance of differences between the HA and LA groups.

The hypothesised consequent manifestations of dream experiences were evaluated by establishing the significance of differences between the subjects at the two levels of anxiety.

The predicted effects of anxiety on speech and language functions were studied by comparing the derived scores between the subjects at the two levels. The qualitative aspects of speech were independently rated by three expert rates (Already described). These experts were all teachers and specialists in the area of child development and family relations. The ratings were pooled to eliminate subjective errors usually present in the rating procedures.

Ultimately, the qualitative and quantitative data so processed was critically looked into, for the presence of significant trends and evidences in support of the major expectations of the research. The procedures for statistical analysis were followed as described by Edwards (1968); Winer (1971).

The next chapter presents the results of the statistical analysis of the data; together with illustrations and relevant comments.

5

Results

In this chapter the results of the analysis will be presented systematically. First, we will present data regarding the initial studies on the tools followed by the final study on antecedent and consequent behaviour correlates of anxiety.

Initial Study

Selection of the Sample

The first step is to define the population from which the sample is to be drawn. From the records maintained by the Municipal Officer, Tirupati Town, it was known that there were 33 elementary schools at the time of the present study. All the children in these schools formed the *universe*. From this universe, a sample was selected *as per* procedure described in the previous chapter.

Age and sex distribution of population is summarized in Table 1 and Table 2 describe the initial sample characteristics on the *same parameters*.

Table 1

Population Characteristics

Age (Yrs)	*Boys*	*Girls*	*Total*
5+	219	201	420
6+	206	157	363
7+	185	143	328
Tatal	610	501	1111

Table 2

Sample Characteristics (Initial Study)

Age (Yrs)	*Boys*	*Girls*	*Total*
5+	25	25	50
6+	25	25	50
7+	25	25	50
Total	75	75	150

The tools to measure anxiety, the anticedent and consequent behaviour correlates described in the methodology chapter were administered to the children in the sample.

We wanted to know whether the CMAS is a suitable test to our condition and yields scores which are sufficiently sensitive. On way of finding this is to study the range and examine parameters of distribution. On examination we found the minimum and maximum scores ranged from 15 to 42.

Table 3 shows the distribution of scores on CMAS demonstrating the sensitivity and suitability of the test to our sample. The distribution is no doubt skewed (SK=2.1) which is not surprising, as it is generally expected to be so in school population on measures of emotions.

Table 3

Distribution of Scores on CMAS for Initial sample

CMAS Scores	*f*	*cf*
15—20	16	16
20—25	22	38
25—30	27	64
30—35	44	109
35—40	32	141
45 and above	9	150

Another way of testing the efficiency of the tools satisfactorily is to examine the patterns of inter correlations. So, inter correlations are worked out. Table 4 shows the inter correlations between the behavioural measures. All the correlation coefficients are significant at P .01.

In order to see whether the items are sufficiently reliable the items have to be subjected to screening by item analysis. This procedure was not employed usually. One other way of screening poor items in a test is to calculate the percentage of subjects in the sample attempting to answer a given item in number of words (TW), Number of Words per Sentence (WPS) and total number of Sentences (TS) for each measure norm are established. It is also important to measure the correctness of usage of language and it is measured by syntax. Syntax furnishes the indication of correctness in three ways :

1. Accuracy of words usage,
2. accuracy of word endings, and
3. accuracy of punctuations.

The aspects measured are syntax; grammatical construction, certain morphological factors and punctuations but scored as errors of word usage; word endings and punctuations constituting the error categories. The error types are indicated as omissions, substitutions and word order. Both error categories and error types are tabluated in the record form and the final score in a complex referred to as the syntax quotient. According to Myklebust (1970), syntax indicates the correctness interpreted in terms of its influence on meaning. The implication here is that the average child attains the adult proficiency in correct usage of written language when he attains approximately the 4th grade level of educational achievement.

The meaning part is measured by the abstract conerete. The concepts formed and expressed by the child are measured. The scores were converted into sten, percentiles and equated with chronological as well as mental ages. The test has been standardised on 847 children. The test is found to be useful in the following clinical and educational situations.

1. As a diagnostic instrument to study children of language disorders and types of learning disorders,

2. As a research tool to investigate the relationship between written language, and aspects of behavior such as intelligence,

Table 4

Inter correlations Between the Behaviour Measures

	Behavioural measures		
	CMAS	*Dream check list (DCL)*	*Family Questionnaire (FS & TBQ)*
Dream check list (DCL)	0.25	—	—
Family Questionnaire (FS & TBQ)	0.15	0.54	—

the expected manner. In such an analysis we can discover items which are either answered by a large number of subjects or omitted due to felt difficulties. Items belonging to second category material have to be eliminated. We adapted this procedure. In our case three such items detected were thus eliminated. After this screening, the final form of CMAS consisted of 50 items (40 test items and 10 L-Scale items).

The family structure and tension balance questionnaire was also edited in the similar fashion. Items 3, 6, 10, 13, 14, 20, 27, 28, 30 were answered by less than twenty per cent of the children in our sample hence were removed.

The PARI consisted of 23 subscales. It is rather unwiedly to use these scores on all the 23 sub scales and further in the absence of data on Indian sample, interpretation becomes dubious. In order to overcome this defect it was decided to factor analyse these scales using the principle component analysis and varimax solution.

Such an analysis in addition to providing information regarding the factorial structure also makes an economical interpretation with less number of factors. Accordingly the data on PARI was factor analysed using the scientific sub-routine programme on IBM 370 computer at Computer Centre, Indian Institute of Technology, Madras.

The factor analysis yielded factors which were labelled A, B, C, D. It is proposed to compare the profiles of parents of HA and LA children on these second order factors.

Another way of evaluating the tools for their efficiency is calculating their reliability. Split half reliability coefficients were calculated for CMAS. dream checklist and family structure and tension balance questionnaires. The following are the values.

CMAS (r=.8); Dream cheklist (r=.9) FS & TBQ (r=.4).

The corrected (SB) values of the reliabilities for the tools mentioned were as follows :

CMAS .88; Dream check list .94; FS & TBQ .57.

These reliability coefficients were sufficiently high and therefore accepted.

The test picture (Fig 1) for speech and language function analysis was modified and developed on the basis of Myklebust picture story language test (Myklebust, 1970).

The following criteria formed the basis for selection of the test picture.

1. It must portray action of a type that provokes as much interest and motivation as possible;

Fig. 1: The Test Picture used for Speech and Languare function analysis.

2. It must be appealing to children of school age;

3. It must lend itself to imaginative thinking and be conducive to speak about more than what is portrayed;

4. There should be a definite' fore ground' and 'back ground';

5. The size of the picture must be standardised and large enough to permit easy viewing by holding on the realising distances, The best size would be 10 1/2" × 13 1/2".

The test picture was developed in the following fashion. A number of play materials were selected and arranged to serve as a back drop. In the foreground a child is provided with few play materials and instructed to play. A number of photographs of this scenario was taken. Three different children were tried to serve as the foreground to realise the best. The photograph in Fig. 1 is the final one which was found to approximate to the criteria described above. In addition, this particular photograph elicited maximum response from children.

The test was administered following the precautions and instructions for administration described in the previous chapter. The speech response was audio taped. The working format for scoring the parameters was also developed.

Final Study

A sample of 300 children from the same population of elementary schools, was selected following the procedure described in Chapter IV.

Table 5, summarizes the age and sex characteristics of the final sample.

Table 5

Sample Characteristics (Final Study)

Age (Yrs)	*Boy*	*Girls*	*Total*
5+	50	50	100
6+	50	50	100
7+	50	50	100
Total	150	150	300

The tools for the assessment (revised varimax) of antecedent and consequent variables were administered to the final sample. The distribution of scores are shown in Table 6. The maximum and minimum CMAS scores have ranged (as can be seen in Table 6) between 10 and 40.

Table 6

Distribution of CMAS Scores (Final Sample)

CMAS Scores	*f*	*cf*
10—15	13	13
15—20	61	74
20—25	63	137
25—30	108	245
30—35	52	297
35—40	3	300

The mean and SD of the distribution of scores on CMAS and scores on antecedent and consequent behavioural correlates were computed. Table 7 summarizes the mean and SD's obtained on the variables.

Table 7

Mean and SD of the Behavioural Measures

Behavioural measures	*Mean (N = 300)*	*SD*
Anxiety		
CMAS	24.61	5.03
L-Scale	5.05	0.409
Antecedent Behavioural measures		
Family Questionnaire	31.34	27.37
Consequent Behavioural measures		
Dream Check list	8.55	2.80
Total words	14.85	11.67
Total sentences	4.16	3.98
Words per sentence	2 69	2.23
Syntax Quotient	67.09	36.20

After knowing the means and SD's we wanted to examine the effect of age, sex and social class variables on anxiety. The analysis of variance was therefore performed on the data using three way (2 × 3 × 4) classification. Table 8 summarizes the results of analysis of variance.

This table shows that main effects due to age, sex and social classes are not significant. The interaction effect between age and social class and triple interaction effect were significant. $F = 2.507$; $df\,(6,276)$; P .01; $F = 3.436$; $df\,(6,276)$; P .01.

Table 8

Anova : CMAS Scores

Source	*df*	*SS*	*MS*	*F*	*P*
Sex (A)	1	19.125	19.125	0.827	NS
Age (B)	2	129.061	64.530	2.79	NS
Social Class (C)	3	180.520	50.140	2.16	NS
A × B	2	25.902	12.951	0.56	NS
A × C	3	58.370	19.456	0.84	NS
B × C	6	287.223	47.870	2.507	.01
A × B × C	6	476.290	79.380	3 436	.01
Error	276	6377.609	23.107		

The interaction cell means are shown in Table 9.

Figures 2, 3 and 4 illustrate the trends. A recognisable trend is seen only in respect of social class, while in the case of others, the trend is not noteworthy.

After knowing that age, sex and social class effects are non significant, the next aim was to find out the difference between the extreme groups (HA & LA) in respect of the antecedent behavioural correlates. For this purpose the top 17% (HA) and bottom 17% (LA) children on the distribution of CMAS scores were selected. The scores corresponding to top 17% were those who obtained a score on CMAS greater than 30 and the bottom 17% were those who obtained a score on CMAS less than 16—Applying this cut off point, there were 40 subjects in the two groups (top and bottom 17%).

The purpose was to find out whether HA and LA children differed significantly on the behavioural measures.

Table 9

CMAS Mean Scores in Interaction Cells

Sex (A) × Age (B) × Social Class (C) (2 × 3 × 4)

Special Class (C)		C_1		C_2		C_3		C_4		*(ii)*
		A_1	A_2	A_1	A_2	A_1	A_2	A_1	A_2	*Mean Age*
	B_1	24.25	26.50	23.57	28.00	22.68	24.62	23.82	25.04	24.81
Age (B)	B_2	25.66	23.33	24.25	22.22	26.41	26.13	23.09	25.85	24,61
	B_3	32.50	29.50	25.88	25.07	23.45	24.20	23.36	26.92	26.32
(i) Mean (Sex)		27.47	26.44	24.56	25.09	24.18	24.98	23.42	25.93	
(ii) Mean			26.95		24.82		24.58		24.67	

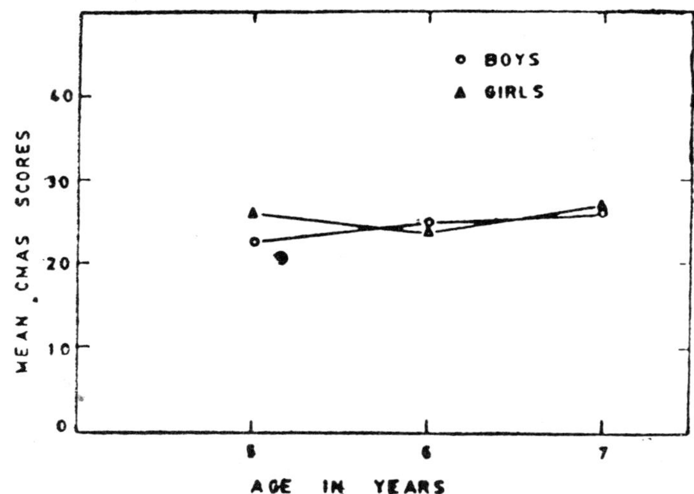

Fig. 2: Age trends in mean anxiety scores for boys and girls in the main sample.

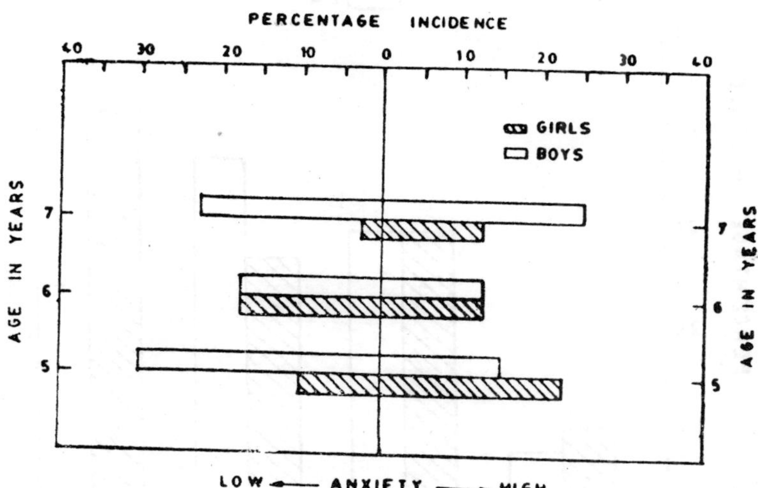

Fig. 3: Percentage incidence of boys and girls HA and LA at three age levels.

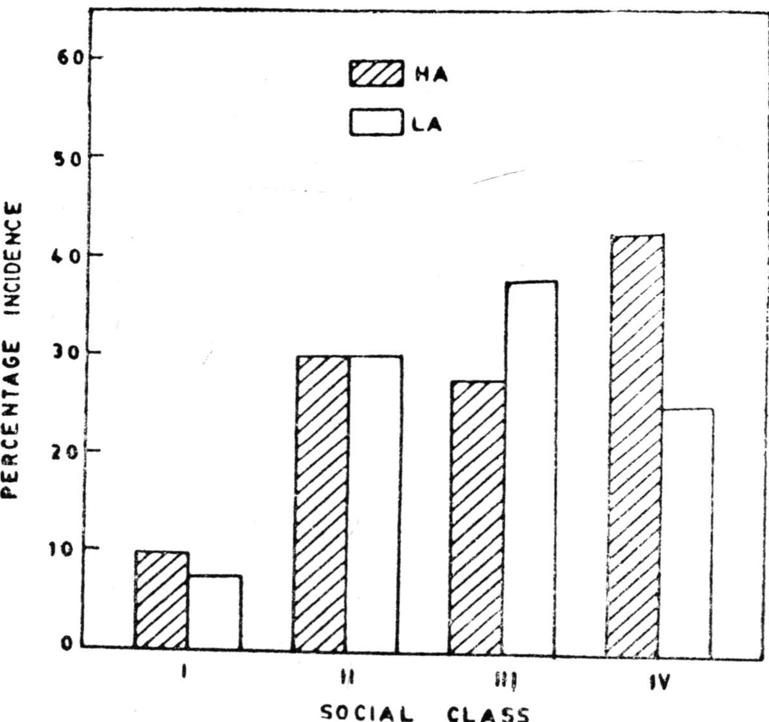

Fig. 4: Bar diagram showing the percentage incidence of two groups (HA and LA) of children in relation to social class.

The mean and SD's in respect of CMAS, antecedent and consequent behavioural measures were computed for HA and LA groups separately and '*t*' test was applied on the observed differences. Table 10 presents the data. Except in the

Table 10

Mean (SD) 't' values for the Behavioural Measures

Behavioural Measure	Group HA n = 40	Group LA n = 40	'*t*'	*P*
Anxiety				
CMAS	31.69 (2.57)	16.65 (3.12)	2.33*	.01
L-Score	5.10 (1.82)	4.05 (4.47)	5.36**	.01
Antecedent Behavioural Measure				
Family Tension	34.85 (21.29)	30.12 (34.29)	4.33**	.01
Consequent Behavioural Measures				
Dream check list	8.20 (4.56)	7.80 (8.70)	3.76**	.01
Total words	17.80 (18 07)	16.50 (23 05)	1.65**	NS
Total Sentences	4.41 (3.37)	5.95 (6.40)	3.74**	.01
Words per Sentence	3.54 (0.27)	3.50 (3.16)	7.86**	.01
Syntax Quotient	77.89 (14 56)	77.90 (47 10)	5.61**	.01

Note : *The '*t*' value is obtained for the difierence between the means.

**The '*t*' values are obtained for the difference between the standard deviations shown in the paranthesis.

case of CMAS scores, the differences in respect of the SD's of antecedent and consequent behavioural measures were significant. Therefore it was decided to test the significance of differences between the means of CMAS scores. Since the variances were not found to be homogeneous (differences between SD's found to be significant), the means were evaluated by 't' test applicable to the case where $n_1 = n_2 = n$ and with heterogeniety of variance (Edwards 1968, p, 104).

The above information reveals significant differences in the variability of scores. It is reasonable to expect HA group to be relatively more homogenous (less variability) than LA group because the subjects in HA group are all high on anxiety and if the effects of anxiety are similar than the consequent changes in behaviour also will be similar in intensities uniformly across the subjects.

With gegard to the family antecedent variables we have some information about the family structure or patterns for each child belonging to the HA and LA groups. The FS & TBQ yielded five different patterns such as Husband dominance, Wife dominance etc. For each one of these patterns, mean percentage of items (on which the typical patterns of decisions are made) are obtained. Thus we have two sets of mean percentage of items; one value belonging to the HA group and another belonging to the LA group. Table 11 shows mean values. One way analysis of variance (within the column Vs between) revealed significant 'F' value F=6.87, df (1, 4) *P* .05. Looking into the means in Table 11, there is observable difference between the two groups, in respect of most of the family patterns. However, there are certain differences in respect of family patterns: which are difficult to explain.

It is thought better to study, the number of children who would be assigned to one of the family patterns; than merely compare the mean values. Therefore, we computed the frequencies of children in HA and LA group; who could be assigned to one of the five family patterns. Table 12 shows the obtained frequencies.

Table 11

Mean Percentage of Items on which Husband, Wife or Both Make Decisions Activities According to the Expected Way Relevant to Each Family Pattern

Family Pattern	*Group*	
	HA (*n*=40)	*LA* (*n*=40)
1. Husbard Dominance	17.80	21.18
2. Wife Dominance	4.35	5.71
3. Autonomous	19.61	24.87
4. Syncratic Cooperative	5.21	3.45
5. Syncratic Division of Functions	31.88	35.46

Table 12

Frequencies of HA and LA Children in Different Family Patterns

Family Pattern	*Group*	
	HA (*n*=40)	*LA* (*n*=40)
Husband dominance	12	6
Wife dominance	—	—
Autonomous	11	9
Synocratic division of functions	17	25
Syncratic cooperative	—	—

Note : The type of family pattern to which a child belongs is decided upon the highest percentage of items on which husband, wife or both make decisions according to the expected formula.

The observed frequencies differ considerably between the two groups of children. The data is quite interesting and suggests the involvement of family patterns in one way or another, as an antecedent variable in determining the levels of anxiety. One of the pertinent aspects of intrafamily variables which has acquired a lot of significance in the recent times is birth order and family size. They have to be considered together, as one telescopes into the other. The birth order is defined as the ordinal position among all the siblings in the family. The terms family size is used to denote the total number of individuals within the family excluding the extended members, that is to say parents and their children only. We wanted to examine the incidence of birth order and family size between the two groups of HA and LA children. Therefore frequencies and percentages of incidence of both birth order and family size were calculated. To serve as a baseline comparison, the percentage incidence of these two were also calculated for the entire sample. In order to see the general trends in the variations they were graphically represented (Figs. 5 & 6). The figures have revealed perceptible differences in the trends.

The next antecedent variable in our list is parental attitudes. The tool PARI consisted of 23 subscales which when factor analyzed yielded four second order factors named A, B, C and D. In the principle component analysis constant used to decide the number of eigen values to retain was 1.0. All the factor loadings 0.30 were selected for inclusion in interpretation of a factor. The percentage of variance accounted by each factor as follows: A, 22.6; B, 26.9; C, 31.8; D, 18.7. In order to study the score of parental attitudes we computed the mean scores for each one of the factors in respect of HA & LA groups of children in the sample. Table 13 presents the mean values, SDs within

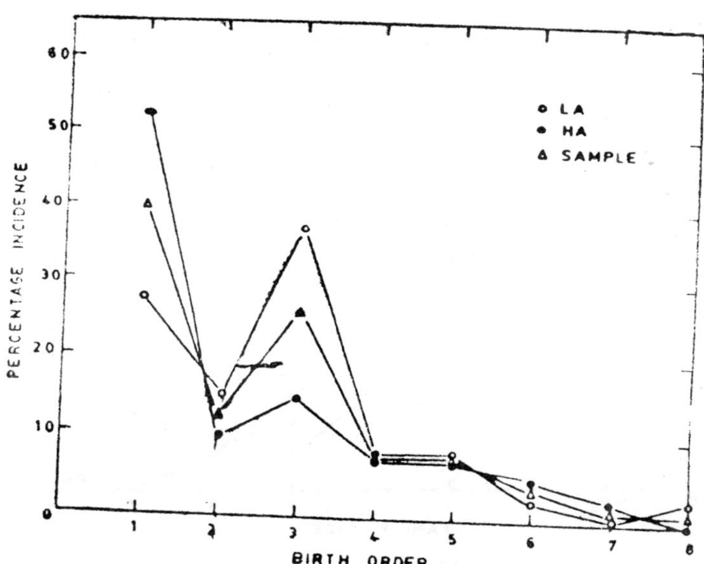

Fig. 5: Percentage incidence of birth order in the total sample and the relative variations in the incidence of subjects of two extreme anxiety levels.

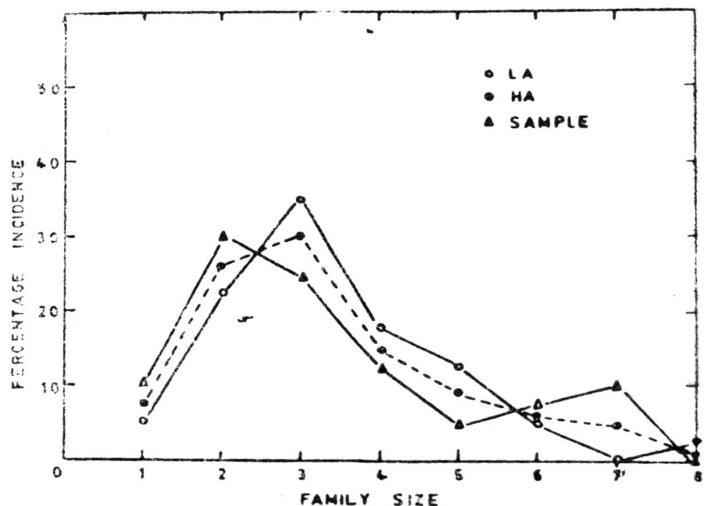

Fig. 6: Percentage incidence of family size in the total sample and the relative variations in the incidence of two extreme anxiety levels.

Table 13
Factor Mean (SD) of the Subjects in the two Groups and the Levels of Significance of the Difference

PARI Factors	*Groups*		*t*	*P*
	HA (*n*=40)	*LA* (*n*=40)		
A	91.73 (26.23)	64.25 (21.54)	1.62	NS
B	85.73 (31.62)	67.37 (26.04)	2.30	0.05
C	74.62 (20.84)	115.85 (32.16)	2.14	0.05
D	57.50 (21.20)	41.47 (15.32)	0.92	NS

parenthesis and 't' value. It is to be noted that only PARI second order factors B and C yielded significant differences between parents of HA and LA children.

In addition to the above, it was decided to construct factor profiles for examining typical differences if any. It would be a laborious affair, if one were to proceed constructing profiles for each child in the sample and still more unwiedly to make relevant comparisons. In order to avoid this difficulty it was decided to pick up a typical child whose CMAS score would fall at 10th and 90th percentile levels on the score distribution and construct profiles for their mothers. Two such subjects were picked up randomly from among those who qualified to be at 10th and 90th percentiles. Next the scores on the second order factors could not be used as such unless they were suitably transformed into standard scores. We decided to transform into normalized standard scores following the procedure developed by Srikant Rao (1964). Making use of these normalized standard scores the factor profiles for the mothers of the two subjects were constructed (Fig. 7). The socre elevations and depressions in the profiles are quite revealing. Further Table 14 shows the mean raw scores on the sub scales of each second order factor for HA and LA groups.

The various parameters in the analysis of speech functions were examined in relation to anxiety next. The data consisted of pooled ratings on eight parameters of the speech functions, for each child in the two groups (HA and LA). The obovious choice of the statistical analysis is to test the independence between anxiety level and the speech parameters as indicated by the ratings. Accordingly Chi-squares test of independence was applied. Table 15 gives the chi-square values.

Excepting for pitch and loudness, all the differences for other parameters were found to be significantly associated with anxiety. Table 16 presents the Mean Values of pooled ratings on each of these parameters for HA and LA subjects.

On inspecting this table the values reveal meaningful direction in the differences. The results pertaining to the language functions are presented in Table 10. We notice that the '*t*' values for the observed differences in SD's are significant, with the exception of the '*t*' value for total words.

The results described in this chapter will be dealt with, in greater details in the next chapter.

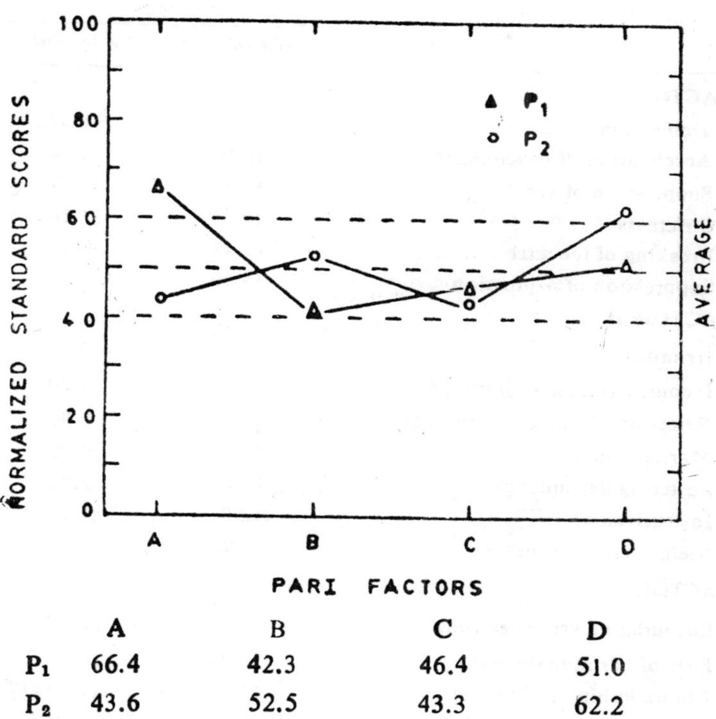

	A	B	C	D
P_1	66.4	42.3	46.4	51.0
P_2	43.6	52.5	43.3	62.2

Fig. 7: Typical PARI factor profiles corresponding to P_1 and P_2

Table 14

Mean Scores on Individual Sub-Scales of the PARI Factors for Parents of HA and LA Children

	Group	
	HA (*n*=40)	*LA* (*n*=40)
FACTOR A		
Deification	15.27	10.37
Acceleration of development	16.00	11.72
Suppression of sex	12.32	11.57
Strictness	14.50	11.00
Breaking of the will	15.42	10.32
Suppression of aggression	15.70	9.82
FACTOR B		
Irritability	11.60	9.40
Inconsideratness of husband	12.70	9.70
Rejection of home making role	11.30	9.90
Maritat conflict	11.90	9.20
Fostering dependency	12.20	9.90
Instrusiveness	11.90	11.20
Seclusiveness of mother	12.90	9.60
FACTOR C		
Encouraging verbalizations	9.80	16.00
Fear of harming the baby	10.20	16.30
Comradeship and sharing	11.80	17.30
Martyrdom	16.70	15.70
Excluding outside influence	8.10	15.30
Equalitarianism	11.30	17.30
Approval of activity	12.50	16 60
FACTOR D		
Avoidance of communication	13.62	10.60
Ascendency of mother	14.20	10.07
Dependency of mother	14.37	10.70
Suppression of aggression	15.70	9.82

Table 15

Chi-squares for Testing Independence between Anxiety and Speech Parameters

Speech parameters	*Chi-square values for testing independence*	*P*
Pitch	0 2772	NS
Loudness	0.2118	NS
Voice	17.4540	.01
Rhythm	23.2470	.01
Fluency	45.9600	.01
Articulatory errors	17.4320	.01
Tension	105.4024	.01
Breathing	41.6200	.01

Table 16

Mean Ratings of Speech Parameters for HA and LA Children

Speech parameter	*Group*	
	HA (n = 40)	*LA (n = 40)*
Pitch	.790	.730
Loudness	.791	.759
Voice	.430	.830
Rhythm	.450	.900
Fluency	.400	1.205
Articulatory errors	.730	.358
Tension	.825	.366
Breathing	.825	.366

6

Discussion & Conclusions

Discussion

This chapter presents an interpretation of the results of statistical analysis of data obtained in the present study, in the light of evidences already reported in the existing literature and reviewed. The results will be examined systematically hypothesis by hypothesis at the same time indicating the possible theoretical and practical implications.

It will perhaps clear the ground if we make a statement regarding the meaning of the term anxiety as used in the present work. It is a general practice to speak of two distinct types of anxiety in the literature namely, state *versus* trait (Cattell & Schierer, 1961), Chronic *versus* phasic (Smith & Venger, 1965), Base *versus* induced (McReynolds, 1967), chronic *versus* acute (Lazarus, 1966). In all these conceptualizations we notice *three* major sources of variance. They are, range of stimuli, intensity of anxiety reported in a given situation and mode of response.

It is true, therefore, that anxiety is not a unidimensional trait, but something that is inside the individual. In contrast, it is a complex behavioural event influenced by situational, personality and response mode factors involving their interactions.

Ruebush (1963) states that anxiety as a 'state variable' is assumed to be an enduring condition of the child that is hypothesized to have resulted from, and is defined by a past interaction of the child and his environment. He says that anxiety is viewed as a chronic emotional state (general trait) of the child which means that anxiety is always with him and he is expected to behave in a different manner ftom a non-anxious child in a particular situation. At the same time anxiety is also viewed by others as a predispositional 'state' variable, which means that an anxious child is not anxious always, but has a tendency to become anxious in certain specific situations. Holding on to this point of view, we have preferred to employ a *state variable measure*, of anxiety in our present investigation.

Age, Sex and Social Class

Among the several demographic variables *age*, *sex* and *social class* are most commonly used in social science research. The reasons are many. To mention a few, an individdual's behaviour in a social situation is caused by a complex interaction of beliefs, opinions, values and roles within a cultural setting. A person's age, sex and social class level are therefore logically crucial ones for any consideration of the possible effects on behaviour patterns.

The three terms age, sex and social class in addition to their general English meaning, connote psychological and social interpretations in terms of specific attitudes and roles assigned within the context of social environment.

Anxiety being a complex behavioural variable is no exception to this rule. Endler and Hunt (1966) after reviewing the meanin? o anxiety have concluded that the issue whether individual differences or the situations are the major sources of anxiety, is a *pseudo issue.* Therefore, it is scientifically untenable to think of a single major source of behavioural variance in the expression of anxiety.

It is only reasonable to expect a perceptible influence of the crucial demographic variables which are critically involved in anxiety behaviour. Therefore, our interest was to assess empirically the manner in which the age, sex and social class get involved particularly in the early childhood years.

Earlier attempts to study the trends due to age, sex and social class in anxiety behaviour have not provided a clear picture.

In view of this fact we have postulated a null hypothesis regarding the influences of age, sex and social class. It is found that all these three variable did not show significantly high effects on the dependent variables anxiety. The triple interaction effect alone has reached the level of significance chosen (p .01). That means the effects of these variables have to be evaluated together in order to delineate the trends. This suggests the complexity of the behavioural pattern representing anxiety.

As a second step, we wanted to compare the mean values in the interaction cells, to detect possible meaningful differences (Table 9). There is a steady (though small) increase in anxiety scores, only for boys as age advances (Fig. 2). Similar age trends for both boys and girls were reported by Dorkey and Amen (1947), Sarason (1958), Bauer (1976). This shows that anxiety is present during early childhood years irrespective of age levels. In this fact is true, the age trends can be clearly studied if large spans are taken in for the research consideration. Children of these age groups can be helped by providing opportunities to work out their anxiety and also by providing proper guidance during this period.

There are a number of studies reporting sex differences in anxiety behaviour. Some studies report that girls are more anxious than boys (Davidson & Sarason, 1961, Muralidharan, 1971; Nijhawan, 1972; Bledsoe & Joseph, 1973; Sandeep, 1975), while others reported no such sex difference (Hollowy, 1967; Murroy, 1968; Morris *et al.*, 1976).

The mean values show that girls at 5+ age are more anxious than boys. In contrast, it is the reverse with boys. The percentage of high anxiety (HA) girls in the 5+ age was larger than boys which gradually decreased as age advanced. On the other hand the percentage incidence of HA boys increased from 5+to 7+ years (Figs 3 & 4). There is a clear cut sex difference which needs to be explained. We may perhaps relate this to girls attaining higher levels of maturity than boys during this age group, hence girls are able to perceive their sex roles even at an earlier age and learn to act accordingly. In contrast, boys learn this at a later age.

Nijhawan (1972) reported that sex differences in anxiety can be explained by two lines of thought. One is that girls in fact are more anxious thah boys and possibly linked with environmental and cultural factors, wherein the stress is more both on household duties as well as academic work. Boys on the other hand are given the impression that studies alone are their primary concern. The second line of thought is that girls easily admit anxiety than boys. This is even supported by Sarason *et al.*, (1960). Anxiety is considered to be a feminine character, so girls do not learn to hide it. Whereas boys though they feel anxious in a variety of situations, they try to hide it as boys in our culture are expected to be bold.

Next possible explanation is that the attitudes of parents and differential standards in bringing up boys and girls.

Parents tend to be protective in the case of girls and therefore they are likely to feel more secure. Boys on the other hand lack this advantage as they are allowed relatively more freedom and are expected to be bold and adventurous. Though cultural and environmental factors constantly expect boys to be fearless compared to girls, this explanation cannot be said to be applicable universally. The liberal attitude and the very expectation to be bold may make boys anxious and often they do not know what to do. Anxiety itself is reviewed as a learned response so, it is possible as age increases boys learn to be more anxious. In modern times there is a shift in the values and expectations and therefore girls are also expected to be bold. We notice that the clear cut distinction in sex roles are fast vanishing even in our country, as a consequence of which many girls are taking on masculine roles and vice-versa. If this is true, it is a complex area which needs further detailed investigation as family values and ideologies are undergoing drastic change.

There is a diversity of opinion about the effects of social class level on anxiety scores. Angelino (1956) found that boys of upper socio-economic group and girls of low socio-economic status reported more fears. Dutt (1968) reported no significant effect of social class on anxiety scores whereas Durett (1969) reported a positive relationship between anxiety and social class. The relationship between high prevalence of psychiatric disorder and low socio-economic status is tentatively demonstrated by Hsu, (1966); Lapouse & Monk, (1958, 1959); Sewell and Haller, (1959); Tapia, (1968). This issue is far from clear. Rutter & Hersov (1977) after reviewing extensively the socio-cultural influences comment that the available data with regard to children's behaviour and development are inadequate in many respects. For appropriate treatment plans there is a great need to be aware of the wider socio-cultural influences and the various ways in which they may operate in a given set up.

The mean scores of boys and girls (27.47 and 26.44

respectively) of social class level SCL I disregarding their ages. However the mean scores of anxiety (disregarding age) for girls in SCL IV (25.93) is second only to the values for girls in SCL I (Table 9).

In addition to the comparison of cell means, it may be worth while to study the incidence of HA and LA children in different social class levels. We expected a differential incidence suggesting the strong influence of social class effect if any. The incidence of HA children is the highest in social class level IV. Figure 4 graphically depicts the relative predominance of High/Low anxiety children, distributed over the social class levels. We notice that the incidence of high anxiety children is relatively more both at SCL I and IV. In the middle range SCL, the picture is not so clear. From this we can infer that possibly extremes of SCL have some tangible effect on anxiety. This requires further probe. The observed results can be understood in several ways.

The low SCL parents tend to be more negligent of their responsibilities towards their children and they may not put enough pressure and provide help for school achievement. It is known either due to indifference or due to economic considerations, children are given sundry work which distracts them. The net effect of all this is perhaps feelings of insecurity, particularly at school and the child feels helpless not knowing where to look for guidance and help. The parents of high SCL children may contribute to the anxiety in their children in a different way. Because of education and sophistication they are likely to put too much of pressure, show extreme concern and lack of tolerance even for a small deviance in behaviour. Thus a child may get into a tenter hook and experience a sense of helplessness similar to low SCL children.

The middle class children may speculated to be safe as their parents enforce uniform and strict discipline. They have also clearly defined goals and expectations. Therefore they seriously learn to prepare for later life. This speculation is supported by Nijhawan (1972), who observed that,

> "the emphasis on supervision and assumption of responsibility arouses early anxiety and frustration but at the same time prepares the child for adjusting to school life and adult life in general".

Though some research on social class and anxiety is reported, unfortunately the data over children is from satisfaction. The only available Indian study by Nijhawan (1972) supports the present finding that middle class children are safer. It is therefore pertinent to state that our results have demonstrated that SCL is a strong antecedent variable contributing to anxiety in children. Particularly the results reveal that both high and low social class levels are strongly associated with high anxiety in children. It may be worthwhile to design, develop and execute shor-term training programmes for parents of both high and low SCL; focussing on the roles, responsibilities and techniques of handling children in the family.

Summing up, on the involvement of antecedent demographic variables with anxiety in children, the present research has found evidence in favour of their possible contribution to anxiety in children. The exact picture is far from clear. Any generalization is necessarily dangerous. Particularly in view of a very small number of studies available. This is further complicated by certain deficiencies in the tools employed in the measurement of anxiety and sampling across different socio-cultural backgrounds. CMAS for instance has some inadequacies. As a very good tool for measuring anxiety in children (Finch, 1974). It is desirable to have more than one tool for measuring anxiety, for a single tool may introduce errors due to inadequate sampling of relevant behavioural demand.

Antecedent Behavioural Measures

Intra Family Variable

Among the several possible antecedent factors pertinent to the development of personality and deviations, home environment is undoubtedly the most important.

By home environment it is meant parental attitudes, parents' beliefs and practices in child rearing, parent child relationships, marital harmony and lack of it (tensions). These in addition to several others, play an important role in determining the course of the development of the child. Winncott (1965) has discussed thoroughly the role of family in the individuals' life. It is only recently psychologists, sociologists and child development specialists are showing increasing interest in the family as a variable and have developed appropriate methodology for studying its effects systematically.

Some of the important findings of the researchers in this area are noteworthy. It would be of interest to know how children perceive their families in terms of roles, responsibilities and power structure in decision making. Employing a family questionnaire between parents, Nijhawan (1972) reported that though both HA and LA children reported tensions, the HA children reported more tension than LA children.

What type of punishments do parents suggest in modifying child's behaviour is an interesting question. The recommendations were found to depend upon parental attitudes (authoritative, non-authoritative), parents' sensitivity to child's emotional reactions and sex of parents (Savitsky & Hess, 1975). In this study it was found authoritarian parents suggested more punishment, were less sensitive to child's emotional reactions, and male parents suggested more severe punishments. Healthy and well adjusted mothers contribute positively to better adjustment among their children. The obverse of it is very much true. Authoritarian and strict mothers contribute to the maladjustment in children (Agarwal & Saxena, 1978).

It is logical therefore to ask what type of parents and family antecedents, do high and low anxiety children possess? Operationally we have intended to measure parental attitudes, family structure and tension balance and compare children scoring high and low on anxiety scale; hopefully expecting clear and distinct patterns to emerge. Our hypothesis is that there is significant difference between the family structures on HA and LA children.

Let us look at the results we have obtained regarding family structure and tension. There is a significant difference in family tension index between HA and LA children. HA children reported relatively more tension balance between parents than LA children (Table 10). According to the rationale of the tool higher the tension index more the areas of disagreement between parents. This is as to be expected and the hypothesis stands supported. Family tension balance between parents is an important antecedent variable.

Now let us examine the results regarding family structure. What are the possible types of family structure do LA and HA children live in ? There are five possible types of family structures as assessed by the tool namely, (a) autonomous, (b) husband dominant, (c) wife dominant, (d) syncratic cooperative and (e) syncratic division of functions. From our results we find that the family structures of HA children are quite different from those of LA children are quite different from those of LA children ($F = 6.87$; $df\,(1, 4)$ p .05). It may be recalled here that the primary data was obtained by asking the children who does what and so on. Our results show that more number of HA children perceived their family as husband dominant and autonomous (11 out of 40 and 12 out of 40 respectively) (Table 12). LA children (25 out of 40) reported their families as of the type of syncratic division of functions. By syncratic division of functions it is meant that activities of wife, wife and husband decide; activities of husband, husband and wife decide but the wife's activity is done by wife and husband's activity is done by the husband. With regard to type of family structure it is desirable to have the type of syncratic division of functions. The reasons are obvious. Using the same tool, Nijhawan (1972) reported no significant differences family structures between HA and LA children.

It may be seen that our results lend support to our hypothesis that HA children report more tension, and in addition there is significant difference in the family structures, using the same tool Nijhawan (1972) reported no significant difference in family structures between HA and LA children.

Birth Order anu Family Size

Next in importance to family structure is the family size and birth order. There is considerable evidence regarding birth order effects and family size effects on the intellectual development. The first born often meets the teacher's expectation and more susceptible to social pressures and is more sensitive to tension producing situations (Bradley, 1968). Ordinal position is not related to reasoning and special abilities (Merjorie Banks & Welderg, 1972). First borns always scored better on Ravens' progressive matrices test (board form) than latter borns. With few inconsistencies there was a gradient of declining scores with increasing birth order. As family size increased, scores on Raven's progressive matrices test decreased (Belmont & Manolla, 1973). Birth order effects verbal achievement and these are not caused either by population biases or socio-economic status differences (Breland, 1973).

It is reasonable therefore to expect similar effects on the personality development but research evidence is not consistent and uniform. In the psycho analytical theories of personality, Alfred Adler (1952) has clearly formulated the importance of family environment on the development of personality, based on his clinical observations. According to Adler (1952) the oldest child is conservative, second child goes along, wants to equal an elder child and feels always forward. Families with larger number of children, who have already grown up before another is born, the last child himself is paradoxically in the position of first child. The last child gets the best attention some times.

Attempts made to relate birth order and family size to incidence of psychiatric disturbances have once again not yielded a clear picture. The mean anxiety scores of first born were significantly different from the middle born and later born (Singh, 1972). The first born child tends to be more anxious than later born children with certain exceptions. The last born child in a family of four or more children tends to be more anxious than the first born (Bharathi & Venkatramaiah, 1976).

Against this background we have decided to look into our data to see whether some consistent pattern would emerge in terms of birth order and family size gradients. For this purpose the data was reclassisfied and graphically represented (Figs. 5 & 6), showing birth order and family size against percentage incidence both in general sample as well as in the experimental groups (HA & LA). No further quantitative analysis was envisaged except to draw inferences from the trends observable in the gradients. There is some difference in the pattern of incidence of birth order in the experimental groups, particularly it is noticed that the third birth order is most incident in the LA group while the first borns are more in the HA group Obviously it means that the first born is the sufferer. This fits into the Adlarian interpretation of the birth order and susceptibility to psychiatric disturbances.

Similarly in the gradient of family size there is a very clear out trend. The curve is shifted towards the larger family size for HA group. There is a shift in the peak towards the left side for the LA group. Smaller family size ground two and larger families around seven seem to be more hazardous; because the peaks in the incidence are found around these values in the case of HA children. Whereas for LA children, the peak is around three and there after incidence decreases as family size increases. These trends cannot be taken seriously because of sampling inadequacies. If this aspect needs to be investigated specifically a proportionate sample will have to be taken and the data analysed using suitable design. This was not contemplated in this study.

Parental Attitudes

Considerable research evidence has been accumulated over the years regarding parents' beliefs, attitudes and methods of handling children. The development of PARI has further augmented research in this direction. Clinical observations of children with behavioural problem also clearly indicated the importance of the parents' attitudes towards children.

It was our desire to examine the parental attitudes as measured by PARI in so far as they contribute to the anxiety behaviour in children. Accordingly a hypothesis was framed viz., *Parental attitude is an important antecedent determinant of anxiety*. In order to evaluate the hypothesis we constructed the PARI factor profiles for the parents of typical HA and LA children (two children at 10th and 90th percentile on CMAS scores are chosen and the profiles of their mothers are constructed. The purpose was to discern significant profile differences between the two chosen parents. Our results have pointed out that mother of HA children differed significantly from mother of LA children on PARI factor profiles (Fig. 7) on factors D and C 5 t = 2.3 *df* (78 *P* .05): t = 2.14 *df* (78) *P* .05 respectively. Mothers of HA children scores high on the subscales such *deification, acceleration of development, suppression of sex, strictness, breaking the will, irritability and complain about the inconsiderateness of the husband and more marital conflicts*' The parents of LA children on the hund scored higher than parents of HA children on the sub-scales like ***encouraging verbalization, approval of activity comradeship*** and sharing (Table 14). The results of the present study are supported by the findings of Agarwal, Saxena & Singh (1978)l Hussaini (1975), Nijhawan (1972); Pain and Nandi (1974); and Rapp (1961). It is believed that authoritarian parents bring up children who will follow their model when they grow up and this becomes vicious circle. Further these parental attitudes become a major source for the development of problems in children, for the simple reason that many parents may interact with their children in an unhealthy way without being aware of the fact. In other words many parental attitudes operate at the unconscious level and often symbolize their frustrations and problems. Providing scientific informa ion and guidance to parents regarding the importance of proper attitudes about child rearing practices may help in dealing with problem children.

The significant difference and parents of HA children scoring high on factors B and C can be attributed to the fact that in our country, that too in our culture, the parents are worshipped, revered and are looked upon as symbols of authority. Because of this, children have less freedom and viability of interaction becomes narrow and rigid.

Marital harmony plays a major role in the family environment. Marfatia (1971) listed, quarrels between parents, over strictness, inadequate and inconsistant discipline and faulty parental attitudes as some of the commonest factors that cause emotional maladjustment. This is well supported by our results, in that the mothers of HA children differed from mothers of LA children, the subscales on factor B and C such as rejection of role of mother and a positive attitude about child rearing respectively. Hussaini (1975) attributes the parental attitudes, to the difference in the levels of education of the mothers, the number of children, their age and income of their family. Highly restrictive mothers tend to be highly hostile, have marital conflicts and reflect home making role by shirking their responsibility.

We have gathered some evidence in our study to warrant a comment on the significant role of certain types of parental attitudes operating as antecedent variables to anxiety in children. It is necessary, first and foremost to intervene in the family system and bring about modification in parental attitudes through appropriate procedures. Child guidance with facilities to work with parents is perhaps the obvious choice to tackle situations, arising out of the above considerations.

Consequent Behavioural Measures

A study of the consequent behavioural changes, consequent to anxiety should be interesting for many reasons To mention a few, it will provide an insight into the possible path ways in the behavioural manifestations of anxiety. Assuming that a fairly consistent and uniform pattern of change emerges, we can uncover the possible primary source behind such a pattern of change. Secondly the consequent behavioural changes if systematically studied will lead to better methods of handling behavioural problems occurring against such a primary focus.

Despite the recognition of these two forms of human experience as having tremendous significance, our understanding the full implications of both dreams, use of language in the waking state is not adequate to offer scientific explanation. Particularly that dream experiences of children are left unexplored except for qualitative and clinical interpretations. It is certainly relevant and interesting to ask what are the typical contents of children's dreams particularly of those children who have emotional disturbances. What is lacking is a short of normative interpretation relevant to a particular age, and social background. It is true, that such normative information may miss highly meaningful personalized value in interpreting a particular child's experience but this information is certainly helpful in planning large scale intervention programmes for child welfare in terms of primary prevention.

In the selection and measurement of behavioural changes we come across the major problem of identifying and sampling the appropriate units of the behavioural domain. One has to consider special behavioural areas which may be age specific, if the primary interest is behavioural changes in children.

From a wide survey of the literature available we noticed almost every kind of possible behavioural functions being related to anxiety. Such a wide variety of behavioural changes getting into the list is not surprising in view of the generalised response of anxiety. For example, a wide variety of physiological changes have been correlated with anxiety. Among the larger (molar) behavioural functions we find academic performance and achievement (McCandless Castaneda, 1956); pereeption at external reality (Sarason, 1960): anxiety and problem solving (Ruebush, 1960); enquiry and exploration (Hill & Sarason, 1963) and class room adjustment and behaviour (Koppitz, 1976).

Dream Experiences

How does a child express its feeling, emotion though dreams and formal (speech and language) communication. Dreams are referred to as *the language of the unconscious*, and the language a conventional form of dreams communication.

Concerning dreams and anxiety there are two lines of thought. The first possibility is that the more, one is disturbed the fewer will be the dreams (Despert, 1937) because an individual may not be able to work out the problem. If dreams are an outlet for pent up emotions, the obvious explanation is then for individual, this channel is blocked and the emotions are seeking expression through other behavioural modalities, The second line of thought is that the more one is distrubed the greater is the frequency of dreams (Gutheil, 1951). Therefore an emotionally disturbed individual such as an anxious child; is likely to dream more often as, such dreams may offer partial solutions to its problems. The critical point in the discussion of the above explanation is the intensity of anxiety and the strength of defenses available to a person. At initial stages dreams may be defended possibly adequately while at the later stages the defense breaks down.

In the light of this background we wanted to evaluate the quality of dreams and their frequency. Accordingly, a hypothesis was that anxiety *effects the contents and frequencies of dream experiences in children.*

In this study, we are reporting the results pertaining to frequencies of the dreams. The qualitative analysis of the contents is not resorted. It may be necessary here to recall the methodology we have employed. We presented a list of dreams to a child, and asked whether the child dreams of the items. The items on the list were based on an interview with sample of children preliminary to the finalization. The list consisted of emotional, and neutral content of emotionality dreams. The child was asked to report how many of the dream experiences it had in the recent past.

The results showed no significant difference in means but the variability between the two groups was significant ($t=3.76$, P .01) (Table 10). This shows that the HA group children are not homogeneous, with regard to the number of dreams. It is possible that some might lack waking life on the problem in this though their dreams, whereas some other children could not have worked out and this mode of expression was perhaps blocked.

It appears from the results we have obtained in the present study, Despert's (1937) hypothesis may not be true, and children dream about *death of parents, thieves, punishment by teachers* and we have evidence that children's dreams center round unpleasant expectations.

It may be pertinent to observe the dream experiences of children, need to be carefully examined both diagnostically as well as a channel for providing support to an emotionally disturbed child in tackling its problem Another aspect of this finding is the need for proper explanation to the children about the content of the dream without aggravating anxiety any further. Parents can be expected to play an important role in this may be a frank discussion of dream experiences of HA children by their parents will be helpful.

Speech Functions

In recent years considerable research information on physical aspects of speech and their relationship to emotional experience have been well recorded. This has evinced considerable interest among psychologists, psychiatrists and acoustics experts to explore the possibility of early diagnostic value of such acoustic analysis of speech samples. Some of the common physical aspects of speech included by well known investigators are *timbre*, pitch, intensity, sound energy distribution (spectral analysis), fundamental frequency or dominant pitch of the cry and amplitude or intensity of fundamental frequency (Broady, 1943; Oswald, 1962; Lester, 1976; Smith, 1977).

One important characteristic of this approach is objectivity and precision in the measurement which has become possible due to instrumentation and computerisation. Some of the results obtained by well known scientists have clearly justified the use of accustical measurements in the diagnosis of depression and other emotional states (Broady, 1943; Kramer, 1963; Oswald, 1965; a Smith, 1977).

Following the above trends in speech analysis it was planned in the present research to examine some of the basic physical components of speech sampled from the subjects as per procedure already described. It is to be noted that the speech analysis was restricted to expert evaluation of the parameters instead of the use of a spectral analysis.

Note: However the tapes containing the speech samples are being processed on a real time analyzer in the department of Electrical Sciences, Indian Institute of Sciences, Bangalore. The results are not yet ready.

In our study, experts, listening to the taped samples rated the quality of speech on a two point rating scale. As is usual in such procedures, we have taken care to eliminate the errors before using the data for interpretation. According to earlier research, *timbre, voice, quality, disturbances in voice, pitch, intensity, rate of speech, deviations in the use of normal words* were some of the aspects of speech expected to be affected by emotions (Brody, 1943; Ditman, 1961; Kramer, 1963; Oswald, 1965; and Smith, 1977).

It was expected that there would be significant differences in the speech pattern of HA and LA children. Voice, rhythm, fluency, articulatory errors, tension and quality of breathing were tested for independence. There was a definite association (Table 15) between the speech parameter and anxiety. (Voicing 17 45 *P* .01; Rhythm 73.247 *P* .01; Fluency 45 96 *P* .01; Articulatory errors 17.432 *P* .01; Tension 105.402 *P* .01; Breathing 41.62 *P* .01). In the rating scale 'O) indicated poor quality '1' indicated average, '2' indicated highest quality of speech functions. The means of pooled ratings (Table 16) show that LA children got twice the value that of HA children for voice, rhythm and fluency, depicting the LA children's voice as more clear, rhythmic and fluent in speech. (Voice, HA=430, LA=830; Rhythm, HA=45, LA=95; Fluency, HA=40, LA=1.205).

The mean values for articulatory errors, tension and breathing, were more for HA children than LA children, (a) HA .730, LA .358, (b) HA .825, LA .366, (c) HA .825, LA 366. This shows that HA children have more articulatory errors, tense voice, and have breathy speech. The results of the present study point out certain practical implications.

1. Experts handling children should not neglect the importance of attending to the speech problems of children as early as possible.

2. Parents and teachers on one hand and the experts on the other, should realise the importance of anxiety, in speech functions and the development of the child.

Language Functions

Language acquisition in early childhood years is one of the most sensitive areas. This is particularly so when we come across a wide variety of language disturbances seen in children. There is enough evidence to show that emotions play a very crucial rule in language acquisition. In behavioural terms language means a system of symbols. The child has to learn the meaning, interpretation and exact sequence in which the symbols have to be used. Stevenson (1972) observes that language assists children in distinguishing objects and in structuring the perceptual field by increasing the distinctive qualities of their stimulk. It follows therefore, the absence of such assistance leads to failure in the proper structuring of the perceptual field and consequent emotional problems. Conversely emotional problems may affect language acquisition in children with the necessary consequences as outlined above. We do not have, at the moment, any evidence in support of this outcome. Bauer, (1976) has offered an explanation to his results in terms of language facility. According to him older children have available, a more elaborate system of verbal symbols than younger ones and therefore they report more fears and dreams which are specific and realistic. The younger children report more formless and imaginary fears and dreams.

We can reasonably expect therefore, the language functions to be disturbed due to anxiety as anxiety has a disorganizing influence. The effects of anxiety on language functions will be much more pronounced particularly in the early childhood years, as the language which are just in the process of development. Bloom, Light, Brown & Hood (1975); Brown (1973); Irwin (1970); Myklebust, (1970) and Perkins (1971) have extensively studied the phenomena of language development and developed the procedures for assessing the language functions.

In the light of this background we wanted to examine the measurable effects of anxiety on certain important parameters of language functions. For this purpose we have selected Myklebusts picture story language test (1970) which gives the following measures.

1. Total words
2. Total sentences
3. Words per sentence and
4. Syntax Quotient

The description of the exact procedure for collecting data and computation of the scores have already been presented (see Chapter III).

Specifically speaking our hypothesis predicted a significant differences in the language ability between HA and LA children as indexed by these parameters. The results of statistical analysis are presented in Table 10.

On examination, it is found that there is significant difference in variance between the two groups for total sentences, words per sentence and syntax quotient (t = 3.74, df (78) *P* .01, t = 7.86 df (78) *P* .01, t = 6.51 df (78) *P* .01). Myklebust (1970) defines *syntax* as something that *pertains to sentence structure—the arrangement of word forms to show their mutual relations in the sentence.* Higher the quotient for syntax, greater a child's ability to master the adult style of language. The mean quotient for syntax were almost same for the two groups (HA and LA). This is so because syntax reflects the level of neurological maturation without reflecting the rate at which the maturation occurs. Syntactical development is complete by 5 years of age (Kessel, 1970). Since the means were almost the same we wanted to examine the variance. This does not in any way contradict our hypothesis as we can always expect wide variation with LA children as against HA children. Unfortunately we cannot make generalisation as the information on children from our own cultural set up for comparisons as well as to lend support are not available. Reasonably to state the hypothesis is relevant and needs further confirmation by specific studies. In our observation in the present research it is found that the language of children is more like that of adult and it was grammatical. Whatever training or modelling is to be provided, it is better if it is given below the age of five years.

If it is true that according to our results that anxiety affects total words, total sentences, words per sentence and syntax, parents and child guidance people must make efforts to remove sources of anxiety from the child's environment. Very often parents tend to blame either the child or the school for language deficiencies without recognizing the real source. It is all the more necessary at this age as some of the common sources of anxiety may be *separation* and *too much pressure*, on achievement before the child is ready. Parents must appreciate the need to handle children's anxieties in a proper way so that the child's language functions are less affected.

Some Comments on Methodological Limitations and Inadequacies

The following comments stem from the present research investigation as a feed back. Such *posthoc* observations following a detailed research study are perhaps expected by way of self-evaluation.

Measurement of *anxiety* in young children is a difficult task. Questionnaire methodology of eliciting anxiety relevant responses has obvious limitations and is affected by well known sources of errors. Even though we have taken precautions and steps to eliminate the possible sources of errors: we cannot be sure of a fool proof measure of anxiety. Ideally speaking, it would have been better, to have included one more measure rather than depending upon a single measure. It would have certainly enriched the information, if one objective behavioural measure of anxiety were included.

Absence of sufficient information on the tool, for Indian children, further imposed a limitation. We have of course, demonstrated the suitability of the tool to the local conditions but this is not adequate in itself, for drawing valid conclusions. The exact determination of the effects of SCL on anxiety behaviour in children, was not possible due to sampling and design problems, (small and unequal observations).

By a careful study and review of the available literature, the antecedent and consequent behavioural measurements have been selected. Some more measures which are relevant could have been included but due to lack of time the list could not be extended. Rigorous psychometric evaluations of some of the tools used for the measurement of both antecedent and consequent behavioural correlates was not possible. For instance the reliability and validity of balance questionnaire (Family Structure and Tension Balance Questionnaire) and speech and language function measures were not specifically demonstrated. The exception of course was PARI which was factor analysed by us. Regarding the other measures the question of validity was tackled mostly on the basis of logical relevance of the contents and some Indian data available. Wherever ratings had to be obtained from two or three persons, we have used the pooled values to remove inter rater variability. We had to interpret the results in respect of these tools under a very serious limitation of a meagre information on Indian samples. Any interpretation under these circumstances, and subsequent inference suffers a serious draw back of useful cross comparisons and generalizations.

In our evaluation of the intrafamily variables specially with regard to parental attitudes family structures and tension balance between parents, only the mothers and children were interviewed respectively. Ideally speaking the other parent namely the '*father*' should also have been interviewed. Further, determination of family structure and tension balance was based mainly on the ehildren's responses corraborative evidence independently gathered from the other family members, would have provided additional supporting evidence.

The question of birth order and family size and their effects on anxiety behaviour is not tackled adequately. For example, the ordinal number of the birth ranks is not statistically adequate as a measure for correlational purposes.

There are statistical indices like Greenwood and Yule (1914) ; and Slater (1962) which take care of the variance in any random population group for valid comparisons. Such indices were not used in the previous research.

Conclusions

The following conclusions are made from the analysis of results and discussion, within the scope of present reserch.

1.0 Anxiety depends upon the combined influence of both demographic variables and social class level.

1.1 Boys and Girls belonging to extreme levels of social class, are more anxious than the children belonging to middle social class levels.

2.0 Among the several antecedent variables, type, family structure and tension balance between parents are crucial.

2.1 Children belonging to family structure with the type of the syncratic division of fuctions experience less anxiety.

3.0 Some parental attitudes are strongly associated with anxiety in children.

3.1 Mothers of HA children are strict, complain about the inconsiderateness of husband and report more marital conflicts. Mothers of LA children encourage verbalization and interact with children.

4.0 The relationship between dreams and anxiety is not clearly established.

5.0 High anxiety in children affects the speech functtions.

5.1 HA children are more tense, show more articulatory errors and breathy speech.

6.0 High anxiety affects the quality of language function in children.

7.0 There is a need for parent education programme in our country and refinement in the techniques of handling anxiety behaviour in children by modifying the antecedent and by recognising the critical role of some antecedent and consequent behavioural characteristics.

Some important suggestions for further research are :

1 There is an urgent need to study anxiety behaviour in young children, especially in relation to social class levels and social and cultural deprivations and disadvantages.

2. Carefully designed, and adequately samples studies to establish birth order and family size effects on anxiety behaviour in children may be undertaken.

3. Further consideration on the relationship between anxiety and school performance, in elementary school children are essential.

4. Spectral analysis of taped speech sample of children who are highly anxious may be extremely useful as an objective diagnostic index at early stages.

7

Summary

Certain antecedent and consequent behavioural correlates of anxiety in elementary school children were examined. Anxiety being a central concept in personality theories is extensively investigated among adults. For reasons not clear studies on anxiety during early childhood years appear to be inadequately emphasized in anxiety research. Information on anxiety behaviour and its correlates in early childhood years is very useful to generate important theoretical implications and to integrate the known facts into a neat explanation of behavioural problems seen in children. Cross-cultural studies in particular provide additional insight necessary to understand the involvement of socio-cultural factors.

The first two chapters describe and review: current concepts of anxiety; empirical studies on measurement of anxiety in children; certain available literature on antecedent and consequent behavioural correlates of anxiety in children.

Some of the current concepts reviewed were; Trait-State conception of anxiety (Cattell & Schierer, 1963); anxiety as a drive (Taylor & Spence, 1953), Mcreynold's Schema (McReynolds, 1968); Epstein's integrative model (Epstein, 1972).

Prior to this a brief resume of the earlier theoretical approaches and formulations namely psychoanalytical (Freud, 1933; Alfred Adler, 1952; Rank, 1952, Sullivan, 1940); behavioural (Miller & Dollard, 1950; Spence & Taylor, (1953); psychometric or factor analytical (Cattell, 1966) were presented to serve as a back ground.

Among the emperical studies reviewed were, studies examining the relationship between demographic variables like age, sex and social class on anxiety; intrafamily variables and anxiety, parental attitudes, family structure and tension balance, birth order and family size, parent's personality; cognitive function (intelligence learning; problem solving etc); school performance, emotional experience (fears and dreams etc); speech and language behaviour and some physiological measures were some of the consequent behavioural correlates investigated selected for review.

After reviewing the conceptualizations and the extent literature the problem of the thesis was defined and the hypotheses were formulated for further probe. III & IV chapters describe in detail the problem hypothesis and the methodology employed.

The following were some of the important hypothesis investigated:

1. The effects of demographic and social class variables on measured anxiety in children are insignificant.

2. The intrafamilial structure and dynamics constitute a major antecedent variable in the manifestation of anxiety behaviour in children.

3. Parental attitude is an important determinant of anxiety.

4. Anxiety affects the content and frequency of dream experiences.

5. Anxiety has a disturbing influence on the speech functions of the child.

6. Anxiety affects the use of communication through spoken language in children.

The scope of the study was limited to the study of the relationship between selected antecedent and consequent behavioural measures and measured anxiety (anxiety was viewed as a state variable) and examined the evidence in the light of the hypothesis formulated. A sample of 150 children (boys and girls) in the age group of 5 to 7 years was drawn from a population of children in elementary schools of Tirupati town for initial studies. The sample was randomly chosen using multistage systematic sampling procedures. The initial study was confind to preliminary evaluation of the tools of research and the procedures to be employed in the final study. Subsequently a final sample of 300 children (boys and girls) in the age group 5-7 years was drawn from the population of children from the etementary schools of Tirupati town. There were equal number of boys and girls at the each level (n x sex x age; 50 x 2 x 3). The sample was drawn following the procedures for multistage systematic random sampling. The following are the antecedent and consequent behavioural correlates examined in the present study:

(a) Demographic variables—age, sex and social class

(b) Intrafamily variables like family structure, tension balance between parents and parental attitudes

(c) consequent behavioural correlates like fears and dreams, speech & language function.

The details regarding the rationale description and the procedures for administration scoring and interpretation of the appropriate tools were fully described in the chapter on methodology. Anxiety was measured by CMAS. Social class level was evaluated using Kuppu Swamy's scale: Family structure and tension between parents were measured by .Family

Structures Tension Balance Questionnaire, parental attitudes by PARI, dream experiences were evaluated by a dream check list; speech and language functions were qualitatively and quantitatively studied using taped samples of speech as primary data obtained in response to a test picture. The contents, format and procedures for the above tools were modified and adapted by the investigator to suit the local conditions. The Parental Attitude Research Instrument (PARI) was factor analysed using principle component analysis and varimax solution and 4 factors were identified and further used in making comparisons. Both the qualitative and quantitative data obtained in the study were processed using standard procedures and evaluation of their significance. To study the trends, portion of the data was graphically represented wherever necessary. Chapters V and VI present the results of the analysis and discussion of the evidences. Both theoretical and practical implications are critically evaluated with suggestions for further work.

The following are some of the important findings of the research reported in this thesis keeping in mind, the major objectives and methodological limitations and inadequacies inherent in the procedures employed.

1. Anxiety depends upon the combined influence of both demographic variables and social class.
2. Among the several antecedent variables, type of family structure and tension balance between parents are crucial.
3. Some parental attitudes are strongly associated with anxiety in children.
4. The relationship between the dreams and anxiety is not clearly established.
5. High anxiety in children affects the speech functions.
6. High anxiety affects the quality of language expression in children.

7. There is a need for parent education programme in our country and refinement in the techniques of handling anxiety behaviour in children by recognizing the antecedent and consequent behavioural correlates at an early stage.

Summing up, some of the significant aspects of the thesis may be stated as follows :

The study has highlighted that anxiery could be measured in young children (5-7 years) and has very important antecedent and consequent behavioural cerrelates. We know very little about the nature of etiology and manifestations; and studies on anxiety making use of young children as subjects are negligibly few.

The importance of family structure, parental attitudes and the environment as a whole is amply demonstrated in the evidences systematically gathered in this research. Both emotional experience and speech a language behaviour seem to be appreciably affected by anxiety. This fact is often missed by parents; and tend to attribute problems seen in children in the above areas to less relevant sources. The present research makes out a case for an urgent need for planning and implementation of programmes for improving parent effectiveness.

Both in the diagnosis and in the development of appropriate intervention programmes for children the need to consider the family environment and to focus on the sensitive areas in child development is well supported. Further studies for understanding the critical involvement of social class, birth order, family size and acoustical changes in speech due to anxiety are indicated from a logical consideration of the results reported in the thesis.

Bibliography

Adler, A., *The Science of Living*, London, Unwin, 1952.

Agarwal, G., Saksena, N.K. & Singh S.B., Child rearing attitudes of mothers of emotionally adjusted and maladjusted children, *Indian Journal of Clinical Psychology*, 1978, *5*, 111-116.

Alexander, S. and Husek, T.R., The anxiety differential : Initial steps in the development of situational anxiety. *Educational Psychological Measurement*, 1962, *22*, 325-348.

Amen E.W. and Renision, N., A study of the relationship between the play patterns and anxiety in young children. *Genetic Psychology Monographs*, 1954, *50*, 3-41.

*Anastasi Anne, *Psychological Testing*, New York : MacMillan, 1972.

Angelino H. Dollin, J., and Mech, E.V. Trends in the fears and worries of school children as related to socioeconomic status and age. *Journal of Genetic Psychology*, 1956, *89*, 263-276.

---

*American Psychological Association Council af editors *publication manual of American Psychological Association* (Second Edition), Washington : American Psychological Association, 1975.

Bauer, H.D., An exploratory study of developmental changes in children's fears. Journal of child Psychology, *Psychiatry and Allied Disciplines*, 1976, *17* (1), 69-75.

Belmont, L. and Merolla F.A., Birth order, family size and intelligence, *Science*, 1973, 182, 4117, 1096-1101.

Bharathi, V.V. and Venkatramaiah, S.R., Birth order and family size and anxiety. *Child Psychiatry Quarterly*, 1976, 10 (3) 11-19.

Bledsoe, and Joseph, Sex and grade difference in manifest anxiety. *Psychological Reports*, 1973, 32 (1), 285-286.

Bloom, L., Light, Brown, P. and Hood, Lois, Structure and variation in child's language. *Child Development Monographs*, 1974, *40* (2), Series 160.

Bradley, R.W., Birth order and school related behaviour. *Psychological Bulletin*. 1968, 70 (1), 45-51.

Breland, M.H., Birth order, family size and intelligence, *Science*. 1974, *184*. 4133, 1092-1096.

Bridges, P.K., Practical aspects of the psychological tests of anxiety in situation of stress, *British Journal of Psychiatry*, 1973, *123* (576). 587.

Brody, W.M., Neurotic manifestations of the voice. *The Psychoanalytic Quarterly*, 1943, *12*, 371-380.

Brown, R. Cazden, C. and Bellugi, C.W., The child's grammar from I to III grades. In J.P. Hill (ed.) *Minnesota Symposium of Child Psychology*, Minneapolis University of Minnesota Press, 1972, *2*, 128-73.

Brown. R., *A first language the early stages*. Cambridge : Harward University Press, 1973.

Buss, A.H., Two anxiety factors in psychistric patients. *Journal of Abnormal and Social Psychology*, 1962, *65*, 426-427.

Buss, A.H., Weiner, M.D., Durkee, A and Baer, H.D., The measurement of anxiety in clinical situations. *Journal of Consulting Psychology*, 1955, 19, 125-129.

Byassee, J. and Murrell, A.S., Interaction patterns in families of autistic children. *American Journal of Orthopsychiatry*, 1975, *45* (3).

Callahan, R.S., Children's Anxiety Pictures, *Journal of Exceptional Children*, 1979, 49 (5), cover page add.

Castaneda, A., Effect of stress on complex learning and performance. *Journal of Experimental Psychology*, 1956, *42*, 9-12.

Castaneda, A. McAndless, B.C. and Palermo, D.S., The children form of CMAS, Child Development, 1956, *27*, 317-326.

Cattell, R.B., The nature and measurement of anxiety, *The Scientific American*, 1963, 208, 96-104.

Cattell, R.B., The clinical factor validity and trueness of the IPAT verbal and objective batteries of anxiety and regression, *Journal of Clinical Psychology*, 1965, *21*, 257-269.

Cattell, R.B., Anxiety and motivation, theory and crucial experiments. In C. D. Spellberger (ed.) *Anxiety and Behaviour*, New York : Academic Press, 1966, 23-62.

Cattell, R.B. Belloff, H. and Coan. R.W., *Hand Book for the IPAT High School Personality Questionnaire* (*HSPQ*), Champaign, Illinois : Institute for personality and Ability Testing, 1958.

Cattell, R.B. and Schierer, I.H., *The meaning and measurement of Neurotism and Anxiety*, New York, The Ronald Press Company, 1961.

Cattell, R.B. and Schierer, I.H. Stimuli related to stress neurotism excitation and anxiety patterns. Illustrating a new multivariate design. *Journal of Abnormal and Social Psychology*, 1960, *60*, 195-204.

Cattell, R.B. and Schierer I.H., *Hand Book for the IPAT Anxiety Questionnaire*, Colarado : Institute of Personality Testing, 1963.

Chomsky, N., *Language and Mind*, 1972, New York, Harcourt Brace, Jovanovich Inc., 1972.

Cohler, J.B., Grunnebaum, U.H. Weiss, H.R.C. and Gallent, A.D., Child care attitudes and adaptation to the maternal role among mentally ill and well mothers. *American Journal of Orthopsychistry*, 1976, *46* (1), 123-133.

Cox, A., Assessment of parental behaviour, *Journal of Child Psychiatry*, 1975, *16* (3), 255-259.

Cox, P.N and Leaper, P.M. General and test anxiety scales for children. *Australian Journal of Psychology*, 1959, *16*, 70-80.

Cox, F.N. and Leaper, M.P. Assessing some aspects of the parent child relationship. *Child Development*, 1961, *32* 637-649.

Dale, R.R., Anxiety about school among 1st grammar school pupils and its relation to occupational class and co-education. *Birth Journal of Educational Psychology*, 1968, *39*, 6-18.

Davidson, K.S., Sarason. S.B., Test anxiety and class room observations, Child Development, 1961, *32*, 199-210.

Devereaux, E., The role of peer group experience in moral development. In J.P. Hill (Ed.) *The Minnesota Symposia of Child Development*. Mineapolis : University of Minnesota Press, 1972, *4*, 105.

Dittman, Allen T., Wynne A and Lymen, C. Linguistic techniques and analysis of emotionalities in interviews. *Journal of Abnormal and Social Psychology*, 1961, *63*, 201.

Dollard, J. and Miller, M.E , *Personality and Psychotherapy*, New York; McGraw Hill, 1950.

Donald D., Anxiety in the relationship of group acceptance to the academic achievement of preadolescents, *American Psychological Abstracts*, 1974, *51* (3), 1973.

Dorkey, M and Amen. E.W., A continuation study of anxiety reactions in children by means of a projective test *Genetic Psychology Monograph*, 1947, *35*, 139-183.

Dubey, R S., Manifest anxiety and educational performance. *Psychological Studies*, 1976, *21* (1), 40.

Durett, M.A., Normative data on children's manifest anxiety scale on Marathi speaking Indian children of different income levels. *Indian Journal of Psychology*, 1965, *40*, 1-6.

Dutt, W.K., A study of the relationship of anxiety with age, and professional hierarchy. *Journal of Psychological Researches*, 1968, *12* (1), 33-36.

Edwards, A L., *Experimental design in Psychological Research*, Third edition, New Delhi : Amerind Publishing Co., 1968.

Elizur, A., Content analysis Rorshack with regard to anxiety and hostility. *Rorshack Research and Journal of Projective Techniques*, 1949, *13*, 247-284.

Endler, N.S. and Hunt, J. Mc. V., Sources of behavioural variance as measured by the S-R inventory of anxiousness. *Psychological Bulletin*, 1966, *65*, 336-346.

Endsley, C.R. and Atkinson, Influence of sex of the child and parent on parental reactions to hypothetical parent child situation. *Genetic Psychology Monogrophs*, 1976, *94* (1), 131-149.

Epstein, S., The nature of anxiety with emphasis upon its relationship to expectancy. In C.D. Speilberger (ed.) *Anxiety : Current Trends in Theory and Research*, New York : Academic Press, 1972, 292-334.

Erwin, M.S. Spiker C. and Miller, R.W., Language Development. In H.W. Stevenson (ed.) *Child Psychology*, New York, National Society for Study of Education, 1963.

Farber, I.E. and Spence, K.W., Complex learning as a function of anxiety. *The Journal of Experimental Psychology*, 1953, *45* (1), 120.

Feldhuren, J.F. and Klausmeir, H.J., Anxiety intelligence and achievement in children of low average and high intelligence, *Child Development*, 1962, *30*, 403-409.

Finch. A.J., Children manifest anxiety scale, reliability with emotionally disturbed children. *Psychological Reports*, 1974, *34* (1), 658.

Framer, L.J., Osterwill J. and Nagi, I.B. Dream, threat and psychoanalytic behaviour, *Journal of Abnormal and Social Psychology*, 1962, *65* (1), 41-47.

Freedman, J.R. MMPI Characteristics of mothers of preschool children who are emotionally disturbed or have behavioural problems. *Psychological Reports*, 1974, *34* (3), 1159.

Freud, S. *New Introductory Lectures on Psychoanalysis*, New York : W.W. Norton, 1933.

Grapp, D.T. and Forsyth, R.A., The relationship between teacher student anxiety levels. *American Psychological Abstracts*, 1973, *50* (5), 9829.

Grapp, F., Manifestation of anxiety in school children, *American Psychological Abstracts*, 1956, *30* (4), 5130.

Greenwood, M. and Yule, G.U. on the determination of size of family and of the distribution of characters inorder of birth from samples taken through the members of Sibships. *Journal of Royal Statistical Society*, 1944, *77*, 179.

Gutheil, A.E., *Handbook of Dream Analysis*. New York ; Liver Right Publishing Corpn., 1951, 1-40.

Gynther, R.A., the effects of anxiety and of situational stress on communicative efficiency, *Journal of Abnormal and Social Psychology*, 1957, *54*, 274-276.

Hamburg, D.A., Sabshin M.A., Board, F.A., Grinker, R.R., Korchin, S.J. Basowitz, H., Heath, H., and Persky, H. Classification and rating of emotional experiences, Archives of Neurology and Psychiatry, 1958, 78, 415-426.

Hamilton, M.A., A rating scale for depression. *Journal of Neurology, Nearosurgery, Psychistry*, 1960, *23*, 56-62.

Hawkes, T. and Roff, R.H., Differences in anxiety of private and public elementary school children, *American Psychological Abstracts*, 1971, *45*, (3), 4886.

Heath, D.H., The phrase association test—A research measure of anxiety thresholds and defense type, *Journal of Genetic Psychology*, 1965, *62*, 165-176.

Hill, K.T. and Sarason, S.B., *The relation of test anxiety and defensiveness to test and school performance over the elementary school years.* Monography. Society for Research in Child Development, 1963, 104.

Hollowy, H.D., Normative data on children's manifest anxiety scale at rural third grade level. *Child Development*, 1967, *32*, 129-134.

Horrowitz, D.F., The relationship of anxiety, self concept and sociometric status among fourth, fifth and sixth graders, *Journal of Abnormal and Social Psychology*, 1962; 65 (3), 156-166.

Hull, C.L. *Principles of Behaviour.* New York, Appleton Century Grofts, 1943.

Hussaini, A.B., Changes in child rearing attitudes of mothers of emotionally disturbed children. *Indian Journal of Psychology*, 1975, 50 (3), 232-262.

Hsu, C.C., A study of problem children reported by teachers, *Japanese Journal of Child Psychiatry*, 1966, *7*, (2), 91-108.

Irwin, W., On language and communication. In, P.H. Muner (ed.) *Hand Book of Research Methods in Child Development*, New York, Wiley Eastern Co. 1970.

Jacobs, J., Birth order and pre-examination anxiety, *Journal of Social Psychology*, 1968, *76*, 9-11.

Joel, B.M. (Jr.), A study of anxiety among English and American boys. *American Sociological Review*, 1955, *20*, 685-687.

Keller, E.D. and Rowley, U.N., Junior high school and additional elementary school normative data for children manifest anxiety scale, *Child Development*, 1962, *33*, 675-81.

Kerrick, Jean, S., The effects of manifest anxiety and IQ on discrimination. *Journal of Abnormal and Social Psychology*, 1956, *60*, 136-38.

Kessell R.F., The role of syntax in children's comprehension from ages six to twelve, *Child Development Monographs*, 1970, 35 (6), 139.

Khandekar, M. and Barah, B.C., *Special Problems of Urban Pre-School Children.* Proceeding of the National Seminar on an Integrated approach to the preschool child, Bangalore. Indian Association for Pre-School Education, 1972.

Kirk, A.S., *Educating Exceptional Children*, Calcutta; Oxford; I.B.H., 1971.

Kitano, H.H.L., Validity of children's manifest anxiety scale and the modified California Inventory, *Child Development*, 1960, *31*, 67-72.

Knower, F.H., Analysis of some experimental variations of vocal expressions. *Journal of Social Psychology*, 1941, *14*, 369-372.

Koppitz, E.M., *Children with learning disabilities—A five year follow-up study.* New York, Grunne and Station, 1976.

Korchin, J.S., Levine, S., Anxiety and verbal learning. *Journal of Abnormal and Social Psychology*, 1957, 54 234-240.

Kramer, L. and Ullman, L., *Research in Behaviour Modification : New Developments and Implications*, New York, Holt Rinehart, Winston, 1965.

Kuppuswamy, B., *Manual of Socioeconomic statusscale (urban)*, New Delhi : Man Sayan, 1962.

Lapouse, R. and Monk, M.A., Fears and Worries in a representative sample of children. *American Journal of Crihopsychtatry*, 1959, *29*, 803-818.

Lavin, E., *The Prediction of Academic Performance.* New York : Russell Sage foundation, .965.

Lawrence, H.C., Common approaches to measurement of anxiety. *American Journal of Psychiatry*, 1972, *48* (2) 3-11.

Lazarus, R.S., *Psychological stress and the coping process,* New York, McGraw Hill, 1966.

Leherissy, L.B. and Oneil H.F., Effect of anxiety, responses mode, subject matter familiarity, programme length on achievement on computer assisted learning. *Journal of Educational Psychology*, 1973, *64* (3), 310-312.

Lester, B.M , Spectrum analysis of cry sounds of well nourished and malnourished infants. *Child Development*, 1976, 47,237-241.

Lewis, A., Problems presented by ambiguous word anxiety as used in psychopathology. *American Psychological Abstracts*, 1969, 43(11), 5908.

Lipmann, S.H., *Treatment of the Child in Emotional Conflict.* (2nd Edition), New York . McGraw Hill, 1962.

Lipsitt, L.P., Self concept scale for children and its relationship to children's form of manifest anxiety scale. *Child Development*. 1958, *29*, 463-473.

Louttit, C.M., *Clinical Psychology of exception children.* (3rd edition), New York : Harper and Row, 1957.

Malmo, R.B., Anxiety and behavioural arousal. *Psychological Review*, 1957, *64*, 276-287.

Maltzman, I., Fox, J.. and Morrisett: (Jr.) Some effects of manifest anxiety on mental setup. *Jaurnal of Experimental Psychology*, 1954, *46* (1), 50-55.

Mandler, G. and Sarason S.B., A study of anxiety and learning. *Journal of Abnormal and Social Psychology*. 1952, *49*, 166-173.

Marcelle, D., A differential study of anxiety (French). *American Psychological Abstracts*, 1974, 52 (5), 5178.

Marfatia, J.C., *Psychiatric Problems of Children*. Bombay : Popular Prakasan, 1971.

May, R., *The Meaning of Anxiety*, New York : Ronald Crass, 1950,

McCandless, B.R. and Castaneda, A., Anxiety in children-school achievement and intelligence. *Child Development*, 1956, *27*, 379-382.

McCandless, B.R., Castaneda, A., and Palermo, D.S., Anxiety in children and social status. *Child Development*. 1956, *27*,- 285-291.

McReynolds, P., Anxiety as related to incongruencies between values and feelings. Psychological Records, 1958, *16*, 57-66.

McReynolds, P., On the assessment of anxiety, by a behaviour checklist. *Psychological Reports*, 1965, *16*, 805-808.

McReynolds, P., *Advances in psychological assessment of* behaviour. California : Science and Behaviour Books Inc. 1968.

Mehribian, A., Measures of vocabulary and grammatical skills for children upto age six. *Developmental Psychology*, 1970, *2* (3), 439-446.

Messer, S., The effect of anxiety over intellectual performance on reflection impulsivity in children. *Child* Development, 1970, *41* (3), 723-735.

Merjorie, Banks K., and Walberg J.H. Ordinal position family environment and mental abilities. *Journal of Social Psychology*, 1972, *95*, 77-84.

Miller, N.E., Learnable drives and rewards. In S.S. Stevens (ed.). *Experimental Psychology*, New York: John Wiley, 1951,

Smith, G.A., Voice analysis for measurement of anxiety. *Journal of Medical Psychology*, 1977, *50* (4), 367-373.

Smith, C. Merril, J. and Mark, R.L., Children's obedience to adult requests—Interactive effects of anxiety arousal and apparent punitiveness of the adult. *Journal of Personality and Social Psychology*. 1974, 30 (6), 822-828.

Smith, R.E. and Sarason, I.G., Social anxiety and the evaluation of negative interpersonal feedback (an extended report). *Journal of Consultant and Clinical Psychology*. 1975, *43*, 429.

Smith, D.B.D. Wenger, M.A., Changes in autonomic balance during phasic anxiety. *Psychophysiology*, 1965, 1, 267-271.

Southworth, L.E., Albert, Z.E. and Gravatt, A.E. Manifest anxiety in economically deprived children in rural Appalachia. *American Psychological Abstracts*. 1974, *51*, (4), 6331.

Speilberger, C.D. *Anxiety : Current Trends in Theory and Research*, Vol. I, New York: Academic Press, 1966, 46.

Spence, K.W. and Faber, I.E., conditioning and extinction as a function of anxiety. *Journal of Experimental Psychology* 1953, *45* (4) 45-116.

Spence, K.W. and Taylor, J.A., The relation of conditioned response strength to anxiety in normal, neurotic and psychotic subjects. Journal of Experimental Psychology, 1953, *45* (4), 265-269.

Srikant Rao, A.M., *Transformation of Low Scores into Percentile Ranks and Normalized Standard Scores*, New Delhi : Manasayan, 1964.

Stevenson, H.W., *Child Psychology*, Chicago : NSSE, University of Chicago Press, 1963, 460-504.

Stevenson, H.W., *Children's Learning*, New York : Appleton Century Crofts, 1972.

Sullivan, H.S., *The interpersonal Theory of Psychiatry*. New York, Norton Press, 1940.

Taylor, J.A. and Spence K.W., The relationship of anxiety performance level in serial learning, *Journal of Experimental Psychology*, 1953, *48* (2), 285-289.

Temple, R. and Amen, E.W., A study of anxiety reactions in young children by means of a projective technique. *Genetic Psychology, Monograph*, 1944, *30*, 59-114.

Thomas, A.C.E. and Martin, A.J., Analysis of parent-infant interaction, *Psychological Review*, 1970, *83* (2). 141-156.

Thompson, George, G., *Child Psychology-Growth Trends in Psychological Adjusiments*. (2nd edition) Bombay : Times of India Press, 1969, 304-305.

Thurner, F. and Wein R., Can anxiety facilitate problem solving ? *American Psychological Abstracts*. 1972, *49* (5), 16331.

Titsworth, M. and Amble, A., Effects of anxiety on perception of word phrases. *American Psychological Abstracts*. 1974, 51 (1), 1889.

Trent, D.R., Anxiety and accuracy of sociometric status among institutionalized delinquent boys. *Jaurnal of Genetic Psychology*, 1959, 94, 85-92.

Triffinger, D.J. and Ripple, R.E., The interaction of sex of teachers and sex of pupils as a factor affecting the teachers' ranking of pupils' anxiety. *American* Psychological Abstracts, 1968, 42 (2), 2976.

Towell, R.D., Anxiety State-trait levels between parents and children in a family practice unit. In C.D. Speilberger and I.G. Sarason (eds.) *Stress and Anxiety*, Vol. IV, New York; John Wiley, 1977.

Uhlman, W.F. and Saltz, E., Retention of anxiety material as a function of cognitive differentiation. *Journal of Personality and Social Psychology*, 1965, *1* (1 , 63-67.

Vishnoi, K.K M., A study of anxiety in relation to over and under achievers. *Journal of Educational Psychology* 1975, *33* (1), 57.63.

Watson, I.R., *The Psychology of the child,* New York : John Weley Inc. 1959, 128.

Way Lewis., *Alfred Adler—An Introduction to his Psychology,* Middle Sex : Pelican Series Penguin Books, 1957.

Winer, B.J., *Statistical Principles in Experimental Design.* New York : McGraw Hill Book Co., 1971.

Winncott, D.W., *The Family and the Individual Development,* London : Tavistock. 1965,

Zilavner, Zand Luz, M., Manifest anxiety in different socio-economic levels. *American Psychological Abstracts.* 1974, *51* (3), 4883.

Zolowitz, M., Essay on interpretation of childhood fears. *American Psychological Abstracts.* 1973, *50* (5), 9335.

Zuckerman, A., *Tape Recording for the Hobbyist.* Bombay : D.W. Taraporewala Sons & Co., 1971, 59-62.

Index